HOW TO PLAY
CARD COMBINATIONS

by Mike Lawrence

**Published by
Devyn Press, Inc.
Louisville, Kentucky**

Cover by Bonnie Baron Pollack

Printed in the United States of America.

Devyn Press, Inc.
3600 Chamberlain Lane, Suite 230
Louisville, KY 40241

ISBN 0-910791-63-5

Table of Contents

Chapter 1

```
J 10 5            A 4 2
          OR
A 4 2             J 10 5
```

For the most part, the combinations in this book will never be the trump suit. They will be either a factor of sorts in a notrump contract or they will be a side suit in a trump contract.

The first important point to make here is the general truism: IT IS BETTER FOR YOU IF THE OPPONENTS BREAK A SUIT THAN IF YOU HAVE TO DO IT YOURSELF.

```
              J 10 5
K 9 8 7                    Q 6 3
              A 4 2
```

If West or East leads this suit, you get two winners. If you lead the suit yourself, you get one winner against good defense.

```
              J 10 5
K Q 9 8 6                  7 3
              A 4 2
```

If West leads the suit, declarer gets two tricks. Otherwise, he gets one.

```
              J 10 5

              A 4 2
```

When you need two tricks from this combination, there are two things you can do.

First, you may be able to endplay your opponents so that they are obliged to lead this suit for you.

Second, if you can't endplay anyone, you have to fall back and hope for a favorable distribution. One such distribution, although unlikely, is to find someone with a singleton king or queen.

$$J \ 10 \ 5$$

$$K \qquad\qquad\qquad Q \ 9 \ 8 \ 7 \ 6 \ 3$$

$$A \ 4 \ 2$$

If you guess to lead the ace, the king will fall allowing you to set up a second trick.

The eleven hands that follow show various problems you might face with this combination. Note that even when the opponents lead this suit for you, you are not always home free. There are often hidden traps. Note also that the combination is not always 'right side up'. Sometimes the holdings have been reversed so that North has South's cards and vice versa.

The conditions of contest for the hands in this book will be matchpoints. Once in a while there will be an allusion to IMP strategy but unless noted otherwise, matchpoints will be in effect. My partner in this book is Alex who played so well in *Play Bridge With Mike Lawrence.*

Hand 1

South
- ♠ J 10 5
- ♡ A K Q
- ◊ A J 4
- ♣ J 10 8 5

After three passes, I get to open ONE NOTRUMP. Alex raises me to THREE NOTRUMP and this ends it. West leads the king of spades. When the defense leads your weak suit and even worse, leads an honor, there is always a little apprehension.

NO ONE VULNERABLE
WEST DEALS

- ♠ A 4 2
- ♡ 9 6 5
- ◊ K 9
- ♣ Q 9 7 4 2

```
    N
  W   E
    S
```

- ♠ J 10 5
- ♡ A K Q
- ◊ A J 4
- ♣ J 10 8 5

West	North	East	South
Pass	Pass	Pass	1NT
Pass	3NT	Pass	Pass
Pass			

LEAD: ♠K

7

I see Alex has been a bit aggressive but I agree with his bid. Opposite a strong (15-17 point) notrump, I think you should raise to game with most nine counts. This one has good points plus a five-card suit.

I also see I needn't be worried about spades. At least not right away. With the king of spades lead, I am assured of two stoppers. This gives me eleven possible winners to choose from.

What remains to be seen is how many of them I can get my hands on.

What dangers exist?

The only danger is that the spades are five-two and that West can establish them and still have an entry to cash them. If West has four or three spades, three notrump will be safe in all cases.

Can I do anything if West has five spades and both club honors?

No. West will use one of the club honors to set up the spade suit and the other club honor to run them. Even if the diamond finesse works, there aren't nine tricks outside of clubs.

What happens if spades are five-two and West has just one club honor?

If I win the first spade, thus guaranteeing a second spade trick, the defense can prevail. When I lead a club, East will take it and return his second spade. This clears the spade suit and West still has his entry. The only time the defense loses out is when West has a singleton club honor so that he is obliged to win the first club trick.

Can I overcome five-two spades with divided club honors?

Yes. If you look back to the previous paragraph, the key for the defense was for East to win the first club and return his other spade. What if he doesn't have a spade to lead? If he doesn't have a spade to return, my spades will be safe and I'll have time to get ten tricks.

The way to achieve this is by the apparently foolish play of ducking the first spade. This is approximately 99% safe. I'm going to feel silly if West has led from Kx of spades, but this is a next to impossible lead.

East plays the six and West gives this some thought before continuing with the queen.

This one I win. A club to my jack loses to the king. West leads another spade and East shows out. I expect three notrump to be safe now for two reasons:

1. West looked rather dispirited when he led the third spade. If he had an entry, he would be more interested in the hand.
2. If West started with the KQxxx of spades and the AK of clubs, he would have opened the bidding.

Correct. I concede a club to East and can claim the remaining tricks. Plus 430.

COMPLETE HAND

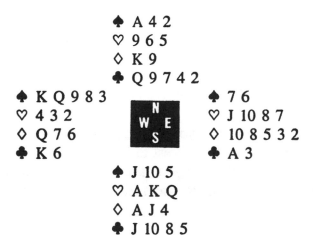

```
              ♠ A 4 2
              ♡ 9 6 5
              ◊ K 9
              ♣ Q 9 7 4 2
♠ K Q 9 8 3                    ♠ 7 6
♡ 4 3 2          N            ♡ J 10 8 7
◊ Q 7 6       W     E         ◊ 10 8 5 3 2
♣ K 6            S            ♣ A 3
              ♠ J 10 5
              ♡ A K Q
              ◊ A J 4
              ♣ J 10 8 5
```

This is the layout I feared and it was necessary to cater to it.

Note that you would not try this play if there were a greater danger.

♠ A 4 2
♡ 9 6 5
♦ 9 2
♣ K Q 9 7 4

♠ J 10 5
♡ A K Q
♦ A J 4
♣ J 10 8 5

If this were the layout, it would be foolish to duck the spade. A diamond shift could lead to you going down on a cold hand.

FURTHER ANALYSIS

A 4 2

K ⟶

J 10 5

With the king of spades lead, you should routinely think about ducking. As long as you trust West to have the KQ, you can always get a second trick since you have the J10 intact to take a later finesse. You will never lose a trick and you may gain time.

FOR EXAMPLE

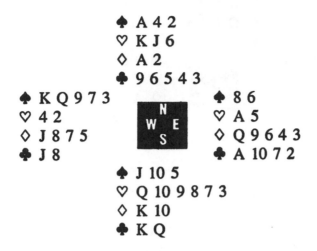

```
              ♠ A 4 2
              ♡ K J 6
              ◊ A 2
              ♣ 9 6 5 4 3
♠ K Q 9 7 3               ♠ 8 6
♡ 4 2          N          ♡ A 5
◊ J 8 7 5    W   E        ◊ Q 9 6 4 3
♣ J 8          S          ♣ A 10 7 2
              ♠ J 10 5
              ♡ Q 10 9 8 7 3
              ◊ K 10
              ♣ K Q
```

In four hearts, South gets the king of spades lead. If he wins and leads trump, East will win and will get a spade ruff for down one. If declarer ducks the spade, the defense can't get its ruff.

Declarer loses if spades are six-one, but he gains if they are five-two and the defense can't get a ruff.

Curiously, if declarer's spades were worse, most declarers would do the right thing.

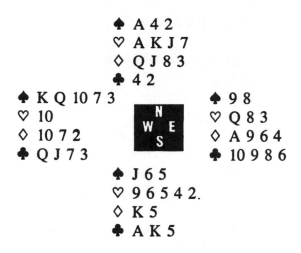

♠ A 4 2
♡ A K J 7
◇ Q J 8 3
♣ 4 2

♠ K Q 10 7 3   ♠ 9 8
♡ 10   ♡ Q 8 3
◇ 10 7 2   ◇ A 9 6 4
♣ Q J 7 3   ♣ 10 9 8 6

♠ J 6 5
♡ 9 6 5 4 2.
◇ K 5
♣ A K 5

Against four hearts, West again leads the king of spades. If South wins, the defense gets two spades, a heart, and a diamond. If South ducks it, West can't lead spades again and must shift. Now declarer has time to set up the diamonds for a spade discard.

Hand 2

NORTH/SOUTH VULNERABLE
EAST DEALS

South
♠ J 10 5
♡ A Q
◊ K Q 10 4
♣ A 10 7 3

East in first seat opens TWO HEARTS and I have to choose whether to act and if so, how. Since game is possible opposite a nine count I'm pretty sure it's right to bid and I can choose from two reasonable bids. I can double or I can bid two notrump. Both are acceptable. I opt for TWO NOTRUMP feeling my hand is notrump oriented. If I had similar values with just one heart stopper, I would double.

Alex raises to THREE NOTRUMP and everyone passes.

NORTH/SOUTH VULNERABLE
EAST DEALS

```
        ♠ A 4 2
        ♡ 8 3
        ◇ A J 7 5
        ♣ 8 6 4 2

            N
         W     E
            S

        ♠ J 10 5
        ♡ A Q
        ◇ K Q 10 4
        ♣ A 10 7 3
```

West	North	East	South
		2♡	2NT
Pass	3NT	Pass	Pass
Pass			

LEAD: ♡4

West leads the four of hearts to the king and I take it. That's
the easy part. I have eight easy tricks and probably can get
another from clubs.

But do I have time? If I play ace and a club, the defense will
clear hearts and when I lead another club (assuming they divide
three-two) the defense will run the heart suit. I have nine tricks,
but they will have six.

There is a chance that hearts are seven-two but this is unlikely
for two reasons.

1. Most players reserve their two bids for six-card suits. If
    they have seven, they open with a three bid.
2. The opening lead is the four. It doesn't look like a
    doubleton.

14

Of these two reasons, I expect the first to be near ironclad until proven otherwise.

Since the clubs won't work, I'll have to look elsewhere. The spades aren't too robust but if they offer a chance I'll take it. Anything is better than nothing.

A 4 2

J 10 5

As noted in the opening section, this combination is hard to play for two tricks unless the opponents lead it for you. Unfortunately, the opponents have their minds set on leading hearts and there is no way I can change this. Since the opponents won't lead spades for me, I'll have to do it myself and I will if I can come up with a combination which produces a trick.

It turns out there are a number of such possibilities.

	A 4 2	
K 9 8		Q 7 6 3
	J 10 5	

———

	A 4 2	
9 8 6 3		K Q 7
	J 10 5	

When the suit is four-three, I can not get a second trick if the defense plays correctly.But if the suit is divided five-two with split honors, I can.

DIAGRAM A

	A 4 2	
K 9 8 7 6		Q 3
	J 10 5	

DIAGRAM B

```
        A 4 2
K 8                     Q 9 7 6 3
        J 10 5
```

In DIAGRAM A I can lead the two to the jack and king. Later the ace drops the queen, Voila! A second trick.

In DIAGRAM B I can lead the jack. If West covers, I can lead toward the ten. And if West ducks, the jack loses to the queen, but the king now falls on the ace. Again, two tricks.

Other less likely possibilities include these.

DIAGRAM C

```
        A 4 2
K                       Q 9 8 7 6 3
        J 10 5
```

DIAGRAM D

```
        A 4 2
K 9 8 7 6 3             Q
        J 10 5
```

In either of these diagrams the ace drops a singleton honor. The J10 will then establish a second trick.

And finally, if either opponent has the KQ doubleton declarer can get another trick by playing ace and another.

Of these combinations which permit declarer to earn a second trick by doing it himself (i.e., no helpful leads from the opponents) the most common by far are the five-two splits with divided honors. (Diagrams A and B)

NORTH/SOUTH VULNERABLE
EAST DEALS

♠ A 4 2
♡ 8 3
◊ A J 7 5
♣ 8 6 4 2

```
  N
W   E
  S
```

♠ J 10 5
♡ A Q
◊ K Q 10 4
♣ A 10 7 3

West	North	East	South
		2♡	2NT
Pass	3NT	Pass	Pass
Pass			

With this auction and with a heart lead, I don't have much choice about where to look for a ninth trick. I should be able to get a second club trick nearly 70% of the time. But I don't have time to try this option.

Therefore I have to play on spades in hopes of a second trick. Even though my expectations are less than 20%, there is no time to try anything else. I have to determine who has the doubleton spade and then play the suit accordingly.

If I am going to play either opponent for a doubleton spade, it is clearly East. There's no chance West has a doubleton spade because that would leave the two heart bidder with a five-card spade suit.

Putting my hopes into effect, I cash four diamonds ending in dummy. Who knows, maybe East will throw a spade away from Kxx or Qxx. This would be a disaster from a defensive

17

point of view. But no. On my four diamonds, East follows three times and discards a small heart. This is good news because East's having three diamonds improves the chance that he will have two spades.

I lead dummy's spade two to my jack and West's king. The heart return comes to my queen and I have nothing to do except lead to the ace of spades and hope for the best. I'm in luck. The queen drops. This gives me nine tricks and I take them.

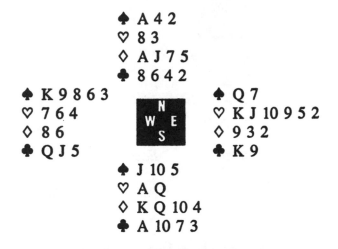

```
                 ♠ A 4 2
                 ♡ 8 3
                 ◊ A J 7 5
                 ♣ 8 6 4 2
  ♠ K 9 8 6 3                 ♠ Q 7
  ♡ 7 6 4        N            ♡ K J 10 9 5 2
  ◊ 8 6       W     E         ◊ 9 3 2
  ♣ Q J 5        S            ♣ K 9
                 ♠ J 10 5
                 ♡ A Q
                 ◊ K Q 10 4
                 ♣ A 10 7 3
```

FURTHER ANALYSIS

If East had gone up with the king or queen of spades, it would be necessary to guess the position. If East had KQ doubleton, I would have to lead to the ace. If East had Kx, Qx or a singleton honor, I would need to finesse. For a variety of reasons, the finesse would be the better play. One of the most powerful reasons is that East would almost have an opening bid with KQ of spades. A second reason is known as the principle of restricted choice. The 'principle' says that if someone plays one of two equal honors, there is a chance he doesn't have the other. This is because if he had the other honor, he might have played it. Don't worry. I've never heard anyone explain this principle in understandable fashion. I don't understand it either. At least, not so I can explain it.

18

Hand 3

BOTH VULNERABLE
SOUTH DEALS

> *South*
> ♠ A 7 3
> ♡ K J 7 3
> ◊ A K 10
> ♣ J 10 5

I open ONE NOTRUMP. Alex raises to THREE NOTRUMP which closes the auction. Brisk and efficient.

BOTH VULNERABLE
SOUTH DEALS

> ♠ J 8 2
> ♡ A Q 4 2
> ◊ Q 8 3
> ♣ A 4 2

```
    N
  W   E
    S
```

> ♠ A 7 3
> ♡ K J 7 3
> ◊ A K 10
> ♣ J 10 5

West	North	East	South
			1NT
Pass	3NT	Pass	Pass
Pass			

LEAD: ♡ 10

West leads the ten of hearts which does no harm but doesn't give me anything either. Three notrump is certainly cold and is the best contract at IMPS. At matchpoints four hearts might be better because there are fair chances of making 620 as opposed to 600. I think Alex's three notrump bid is correct and I hope to make an overtrick to justify his decision.

It looks like any overtrick must come from clubs and if this is to occur I must find an opponent with a doubleton honor.

I can afford to cash four hearts and three diamonds in an effort to get a count and I shall start to do this. I cash three hearts keeping a high one in dummy. West has the 109 doubleton and on the third heart he pitches a small diamond. From this evidence I might conclude that West has long clubs but I don't have to commit myself. I cash three diamonds ending in my hand. I do this so that I can lead clubs from my hand if I so choose and I can go to dummy in hearts to lead a club if I feel that best.

On the diamonds, East follows twice and then discards a small club. This means West started with two hearts and five diamonds. I think if either opponent has a doubleton club, it will be West. Two reasons.

1. West has only six unknown cards to East's eight unknown cards. West has fewer black cards and therefore more likely to have a specific doubleton.
2. If East has a doubleton club, he has six spades. If this is so, why did East discard a club and not a spade.

Expecting that if anyone has a doubleton club honor it will be West, I lead the club jack. I choose the jack on the off chance that West will err by covering with Qxx or Kxx. West does cover with the king and when I return a club from dummy, East takes his queen. I have ten tricks.

COMPLETE HAND

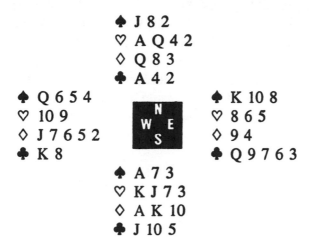

```
                ♠ J 8 2
                ♡ A Q 4 2
                ◊ Q 8 3
                ♣ A 4 2
♠ Q 6 5 4            N         ♠ K 10 8
♡ 10 9          W       E      ♡ 8 6 5
◊ J 7 6 5 2         S          ◊ 9 4
♣ K 8                         ♣ Q 9 7 6 3
                ♠ A 7 3
                ♡ K J 7 3
                ◊ A K 10
                ♣ J 10 5
```

FURTHER ANALYSIS

It was necessary to play the red suits correctly keeping an entry to the North hand. Had I cashed all four hearts and then three diamonds, I might have found myself in, say, the South hand. If my count told me that East had the short clubs, I would want to lead a club from dummy, but I would no longer have the entry to do that.

East made my guess easier by going up with the queen of clubs. I was probably going to guess them but there's always the chance I would not. If I got the clever idea that West started with KQ doubleton of clubs, I might duck the second round. Fortunately, I was not put to the test.

I noted that declarers in four hearts would probably take ten tricks. It turns out they would, but their chances were far better than my chances of ten tricks in notrump. Assuming a safe lead, say the ten of hearts, declarer would draw trump in three rounds. Then the ace, king and queen of diamonds. Now declarer can play the ace and another spade. The defense will be forced to play clubs sooner or later which will allow declarer to lose only one club, or the defense will have to give a sluff and a ruff with the same effect.

If hearts had divided four-one, declarer would not have been able to achieve this endplay and would have been forced to find the same club technique I used in three notrump.

Hand 4

EAST/WEST VULNERABLE
SOUTH DEALS

> *South*
> ♠ A 4 2
> ♡ K 8 7
> ◇ A K 10 3
> ♣ 10 8 2

I open ONE DIAMOND and Alex responds TWO CLUBS. TWO NOTRUMP looks right so I bid it. Alex raises to THREE NOTRUMP and West leads the eight of spades. This could be bad for us.

EAST/WEST VULNERABLE
SOUTH DEALS

> ♠ J 10 5
> ♡ A J 4
> ◇ 9 4
> ♣ K Q J 7 3

```
  N
W   E
  S
```

> ♠ A 4 2
> ♡ K 8 7
> ◇ A K 10 3
> ♣ 10 8 2

West	North	East	South
			1 ◇
Pass	2 ♣	Pass	2NT
Pass	3NT	Pass	Pass
Pass			

LEAD: ♠ 8

It looks like there are lots of tricks here. Potentially twelve of them. Hope I can take nine.

This dummy only partially relieves my worry about that opening lead. I doubt it's fourth best. If it is, the jack of spades will win. I play it and East covers with the queen.

It wasn't fourth best. My decision to take this trick is not clear at all. If West has led from K98, I should win. But if the eight is top of nothing, I could be in danger if I take it. If I win the ace of spades and lead a club, West can win and return a spade. This could actually lead to down one. Hard to believe.

I have available a sure play to make nine tricks. I can duck the queen of spades. If East has KQ9xx, he won't be able to continue them. But ducking costs me if West has led from K98. It won't cost me the contract, but it will cost overtricks.

This is a genuine guess. At IMPs I would duck routinely. At matchpoints it's less easy. To further confuse the issue, if East has the ace of clubs, I can win the first trick and be safe. I'm going to guess to duck. Not because it guarantees the contract, but because I would judge the K98 as not being a very attractive lead. Given a choice of leads most defenders would prefer 8 from 8x than K98.

East has had some time to think about his play as my duck was not exactly smooth. My opinion of the outstanding spades seems right because he switches to the jack of diamonds. I win and attack clubs. West takes the third round while East follows once and then discards the heart two and the spade three.

West continues the spade six. I doubt it makes any difference what I do. East is looking confident and he looks at me as if to confirm my play doesn't matter. I believe him. I duck the spade and take East's seven with the ace.

I have nine easy tricks and must be a favorite for another. I can finesse in hearts, which means I go down if it loses. Or, I can play the king of diamonds, ace of hearts, two good clubs, and throw East in with a spade.

If he has the queen of hearts he will be endplayed. But West may have the queen of hearts in which case I may again go down.

I can also play to the ace of hearts, cash two clubs pitching a heart and a spade and finesse the nine of diamonds losing to the queen. If West has another spade, I get nine tricks only.

But I don't think he does. East made a technical error when he played the seven. He should have played the nine.

Trusting my judgement, I take line three which gets ten tricks when West turns out to have just two spades. Annoyingly West also has a doubleton queen of hearts so that the heart finesse line also worked.

COMPLETE HAND

```
              ♠ J 10 5
              ♡ A J 4
              ◊ 9 4
              ♣ K Q J 7 3
♠ 8 6                        ♠ K Q 9 7 3
♡ Q 3          N             ♡ 10 9 6 5 2
◊ Q 8 7 5 2   W   E          ◊ J 6
♣ A 9 5 4      S             ♣ 6
              ♠ A 4 2
              ♡ K 8 7
              ◊ A K 10 3
              ♣ 10 8 2
```

At least my second line, endplaying East, would have failed.

Hand 5

NORTH/SOUTH VULNERABLE
WEST DEALS

South
♠ A 4 2
♡ A 6 2
◇ A 10 8 3
♣ A 9 2

There are three passes to me and I am more or less obligated to open ONE NOTRUMP. I am not excited about this because this hand has very little 'lead value.' i.e., there is little reason to want to declare this hand. The only suit I can stand for the opponents to lead is diamonds. Both majors are poorly suited to an opening lead and clubs are not much better. The reason I choose one notrump is that these values are impossible to show if I don't bid one notrump. Believe me, it is not greed that makes me do it.

Alex raises me to THREE NOTRUMP and, as on the previous hand, I get a spade lead. The spade seven to be exact. Aside from the fact that my spades are not going to benefit from the opening lead, I know dummy won't have many spades since Alex didn't bother with Stayman. It's true he may have four of a major now and then, but he also can have two or even one of them. By comparison, when is the last time your partner raised you to three notrump with a singleton in clubs or diamonds?

NORTH/SOUTH VULNERABLE
WEST DEALS

```
         ♠ J 10 5
         ♡ K Q 4
         ◊ K J 7 6 2
         ♣ J 4
```

```
            N
         W     E
            S
```

```
         ♠ A 4 2
         ♡ A 6 2
         ◊ A 10 8 3
         ♣ A 9 2
```

West	North	East	South
Pass	Pass	Pass	1NT
Pass	3NT	Pass	Pass
Pass			

LEAD: ♠7

I cover West's seven of spades with the jack and East covers
with the queen. Too bad. Sometimes the jack wins.

I can take this or I can duck as I did on the previous hand.
The spade suit is not as clear to me this time. West can have
73 and he can have K9873. Both holdings are possible and either
would be an acceptable choice.

I do not have a real decision this time because I have a 100%
counter to the defense.

The worst thing that can happen to me is that West gets in
and leads another spade. If East has KQ983, I would go down.
This time I have a say in whether West gets in. I win the ace
of spades and try the ace and ten of diamonds. East follows
with the nine and West follows with the four and five. Percent-

agewise, it is slightly right to play the king. Doing so risks going down if West has Qxx and a doubleton spade. I think that it is right to take the sure line by finessing. If East has the diamond queen I lose a trick but I gain the contract. I also have going for me that if East does win the queen of diamonds, he may not find a club return. If he returns a spade I get a trick I might not have had the courage to go after myself.

When the diamond ten wins I now have a good board but I still have a problem. Should I take ten tricks or should I lead a spade and try for eleven? How good is ten tricks going to be?

If West started with 73 of spades, ten tricks will be good indeed. If West started with K9873, then ten tricks will be found rather often.

Maybe a few more rounds of diamonds will clear up some of this. East has already thrown the three and five of hearts and on the next two diamonds he throws the five of clubs with no certainty, and then the seven of hearts. West throws the six of clubs and the three of spades. I have fewer problems than the opponents since I have only one discard to make.

My first thought is to throw a heart but I want to cash the heart suit next ending in my hand. In order to do that I have to keep my hearts. Also, if I want a second spade trick, I have to keep both of those. Perforce, I throw the two of clubs.

I already think West has led from K9873 of spades because he threw the three. If he had 73 only, he would have kept the three. When I play the three top hearts East follows twice more showing he started with 108753 and then discards the three of clubs. West follows with the 9-J of hearts and finally throws the spade eight.

Now it's clear that I can lead a spade and West produces the king. This gives me eleven tricks and I lose last to the king of clubs.

COMPLETE HAND

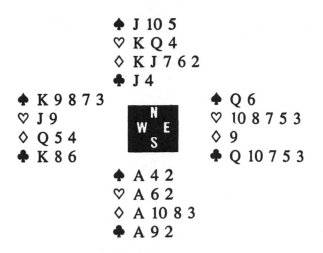

♠ J 10 5
♡ K Q 4
◇ K J 7 6 2
♣ J 4

♠ K 9 8 7 3
♡ J 9
◇ Q 5 4
♣ K 8 6

♠ Q 6
♡ 10 8 7 5 3
◇ 9
♣ Q 10 7 5 3

♠ A 4 2
♡ A 6 2
◇ A 10 8 3
♣ A 9 2

FURTHER ANALYSIS

This hand would be a snap at IMPs. Lock up your nine tricks and run.

Note that on this hand, ducking the spade isn't such a good idea. Letting the queen win would pay off to K9873 and since this is a very possible holding, it would be dangerous.

Hand 6

EAST/WEST VULNERABLE
EAST DEALS

South
♠ J 10 5
♡ K 6 4 3
◊ 6 5 3
♣ A 5 2

East bids ONE HEART as dealer and I PASS as does West. Alex DOUBLES and East continues with TWO HEARTS. This is tempting vulnerability for a penalty double but my heart sports are too feeble. I PASS. It gets around to Alex and he contests with THREE DIAMONDS. This shows a good hand and I have both a semifit and a few values. I try THREE NOTRUMP rather than a nebulous three hearts. Why try for three notrump from partner's side when he is not going to be able to bid it. This is passed out and West leads the two of hearts.

EAST/WEST VULNERABLE
EAST DEALS

> ♠ A 4 2
> ♡ Q 5
> ◊ A K Q J 9 7
> ♣ 8 6

> ♠ J 10 5
> ♡ K 6 4 3
> ◊ 6 5 3
> ♣ A 5 2

West	North	East	South
		1 ♡	Pass
Pass	Double	2 ♡	Pass
Pass	3 ◊	Pass	3NT
Pass	Pass	Pass	

LEAD: ♡2

So much for why I didn't bid three hearts. It looks like nine tricks from my side and ten or eleven from Alex's. Nice decision!

I play low in dummy and win the seven with the king. There may be only nine tricks here but if East has all the missing high cards, he will come under some pressure when I run the diamonds. I start diamonds which divide two-two. As I continue the suit East discards the nine and three of clubs. West discards the jack of clubs and the seven of spades. On the last two diamonds East pitches the queen of clubs and the eight of hearts, West the three and six of spades.

Now what? I can run with nine tricks or I can hope something good has happened.

Obviously I can't afford to duck a spade. East would win and cash four hearts. Instead I cash the spade ace dropping the king from East. This could be good news. It could also be a headache. If East has KQ of spades, I have to cash out. If East has the singleton king of spades, I can lead a spade and establish a tenth trick. Hearts are safe if West gets in because the auction and lead proves them to be six-one.

I'm going to lead a spade and play for the overtrick. Too many things point to this being right.

1. If East has the KQ of spades, he has only three clubs which would be Q93 which he has already discarded. Why would his first discard be the nine of clubs?

2. If West started with 98763 of spades, why did he discard the seven first? Defense is a game of communications. A partnership that sends meaningless signals loses far more than a pair which send honest signals.

3. Finally, it's possible that Alex's hand will play three notrump and with a heart lead there will be ten easy tricks. I lead a spade and do come to ten tricks.

COMPLETE HAND

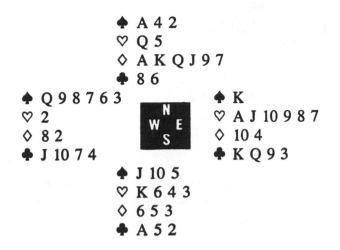

```
            ♠ A 4 2
            ♡ Q 5
            ◊ A K Q J 9 7
            ♣ 8 6
♠ Q 9 8 7 6 3                    ♠ K
♡ 2              N              ♡ A J 10 9 8 7
◊ 8 2          W   E           ◊ 10 4
♣ J 10 7 4        S            ♣ K Q 9 3
            ♠ J 10 5
            ♡ K 6 4 3
            ◊ 6 5 3
            ♣ A 5 2
```

FURTHER ANALYSIS

West's discard of the club jack helped East judge what to discard. Whether it helped on this hand is not the point. Had West discarded, say, the seven of clubs, East would be less sure of the position.

Hand 7

NO ONE VULNERABLE
WEST DEALS

South
♠ A 10 2
♡ 9 4 2
◇ A Q J 3
♣ J 10 5

In second seat, Alex opens ONE HEART. I have tenaces in two suits so this time I'm not embarassed to bid TWO NOTRUMP. Alex raises me to THREE NOTRUMP which is passed out.

NO ONE VULNERABLE
WEST DEALS

♠ 8 3
♡ K Q J 10 6
◇ K 4 2
♣ A 4 2

♠ A 10 2
♡ 9 4 2
◇ A Q J 3
♣ J 10 5

West	North	East	South
Pass	1♡	Pass	2NT
Pass	3NT	Pass	Pass
Pass			

LEAD: ♣7

West leads the club seven which is a little unexpected. This sequence tends to call for a major suit lead and with this dummy I would have expected a spade lead.

This lead is tantalizing me. If I duck and lose to an honor, I will score eleven tricks if East returns a club. But I will score only seven or eight if East returns a spade. What are the chances West has both club honors? I might win the first trick with the jack which would make this an easy hand.

If the seven is a true fourth best, West will have one of these holdings.

$$K \ 9 \ 8 \ 7 \ (x)$$
$$Q \ 9 \ 8 \ 7 \ (x)$$
$$K \ Q \ 9 \ 7 \ (x)$$
$$K \ Q \ 8 \ 7 \ (x)$$

I tend to discount the third holding. West might lead the king from KQ97x. Just possibly he might lead the king from KQ87(x). I think West is about 65% to have either of the first two combinations.

If I duck the club, and East wins, he may return a club but I wouldn't count on it.

Is there any way I can keep East from switching to a spade?

Yes. It's a little unusual but I can stop a spade switch by not letting East in to lead one.

At trick one, I take the ace of clubs and start the heart suit. My hope is that the club honors are divided. If they are, I will take only nine tricks if clubs are four-three, but I will take ten if clubs are five-two because they will be blocked. The only real danger is that West has both club honors. I expect clubs are five-two because West would need a good reason to lead clubs on this sequence. The fact he couldn't find a spade lead tends to deny spade length. This in turn implies long clubs. No guarantees though.

When I lead hearts East takes the third round and cashes the king of clubs.

The moment of truth. Does he have another club? No. He switches to the spade queen and I grab it. Ten tricks later I lose the last trick for plus 430.

This rates to be good because ten tricks would be the limit in hearts with a spade lead.

COMPLETE HAND

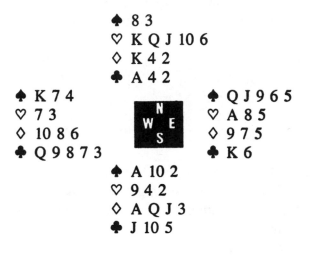

```
                    ♠ 8 3
                    ♡ K Q J 10 6
                    ◊ K 4 2
                    ♣ A 4 2
    ♠ K 7 4                         ♠ Q J 9 6 5
    ♡ 7 3            N              ♡ A 8 5
    ◊ 10 8 6      W     E           ◊ 9 7 5
    ♣ Q 9 8 7 3      S              ♣ K 6
                    ♠ A 10 2
                    ♡ 9 4 2
                    ◊ A Q J 3
                    ♣ J 10 5
```

Hand 8

NO ONE VULNERABLE
WEST DEALS

South
- ♠ J 10 5
- ♡ J 9 8 6 5
- ◊ 10 4 2
- ♣ A K

West opens ONE DIAMOND and Alex DOUBLES. When East PASSES, I have to decide how to express my values. TWO HEARTS seems about right so I bid it. West backs in with a DOUBLE of his own. Alex PASSES and East bids a somewhat sad THREE DIAMONDS. It might be said that I have already bid my hand but I think it conservative to pass. I bid THREE HEARTS. I have a fifth heart, I have nothing wasted in diamonds, and I have extremely good high cards. As an aside, my two heart bid could get Alex off to a bad lead. But this is more a whimsical thought than a real one. No one else has anything to add to this so I buy it at three hearts. West leads the king of diamonds.

NO ONE VULNERABLE
WEST DEALS

```
        ♠ A 4 2
        ♡ A K 3 2
        ◇ 8 6
        ♣ 8 5 4 2

            N
         W     E
            S

        ♠ J 10 5
        ♡ J 9 8 6 5
        ◇ 10 4 2
        ♣ A K
```

West	North	East	South
1 ◇	Double	Pass	2 ♡
Double	Pass	3 ◇	3 ♡
Pass	Pass	Pass	

LEAD: ◇ K

West cashes the king and jack of diamonds, East playing the three and five, and switches to the queen of clubs.

If hearts are two-two or a stiff queen exists, I will make three with chances for four.

If hearts are two-two, there won't be much to do except worry about an overtrick. If I have a heart loser though I will go down if I can't avoid two spade losers.

The one thing I know about the spades is that they are four-three with West having four. This I know from the bidding. This means I must lose two tricks if I play the suit myself. I have chances for an endplay if I can guess the position.

In order to effect an endplay, I have to get rid of the clubs and diamonds. I win the club ace and play a heart to the ace.

38

Back to the king of clubs and a heart to the king. West discards the three of spades so I do have a heart loser. I ruff a club, a diamond in dummy, and lead dummy's last club, East discarding a diamond. When I ruff this we are down to a four-card position with South on lead. At this point, West is down to three spades and a diamond. East has three spades and the queen of hearts.

North
♠ A 4 2
♡ 3
◊ —
♣ —

South
♠ J 10 5
♡ J
◊ —
♣ —

If West has both honors, I have to lead the jack and duck when West covers. He will be forced to lead away from his spade honor or give a sluff and a ruff.

If I think East has a spade honor I have to put East in with a heart. He will have to break spades for me. Ok. What's the right guess?

A

West	East
♠ K 9 8 3	♠ Q 7 6
♡ 10	♡ Q 7 4
◊ A K Q J	◊ 9 7 5 3
♣ Q J 10 3	♣ 9 7 6

B

West	East
♠ K Q 9 3	♠ 8 7 6
♡ 10	♡ Q 7 4
◊ A K Q J	◊ 9 7 5 3
♣ Q J 10 3	♣ 9 7 6

Which combination exists, A or B?

If West had A, he would bid as he did. It is certainly a possible hand. It occurs to me that in combination A, the king and queen of spades may be interchanged. I think if this is so that West would still have his bids.

If combination B exists I think West might have thought longer over my three hearts. This would sway me slightly in favor of hand A. There is another clue though which suggests hand B. During the auction, East's emotions ranged from bored when he picked his hand up to pained when he bid three diamonds. I guarantee East does not like his hand. I wonder if East is good enough to know that hand A with its queen (or king) of spades is actually an OK hand.

Finally, there is a clue which should be one hundred percent if I could trust my opponents to know what they are doing. If East has Qxx of spades, he could beat me by throwing a small spade when I ruffed the last club rather than his diamond. I wouldn't be able to pick up the spades with one loser because East would get in with the queen, draw trump, and cash his diamond.

The trouble is that I don't know these opponents and don't know if they are competent.

Since West can have the king and queen of spades, I'll play for it since I can succeed against it.

I lead the spade jack and duck when West covers with the queen. He returns a small spade and I finesse it to my ten, winning.

Nine nervous tricks.

COMPLETE HAND

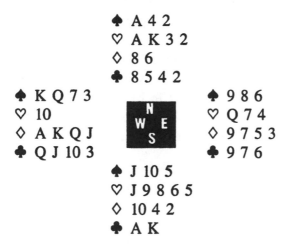

```
              ♠ A 4 2
              ♡ A K 3 2
              ◇ 8 6
              ♣ 8 5 4 2
 ♠ K Q 7 3                    ♠ 9 8 6
 ♡ 10              N          ♡ Q 7 4
 ◇ A K Q J      W   E         ◇ 9 7 5 3
 ♣ Q J 10 3        S          ♣ 9 7 6
              ♠ J 10 5
              ♡ J 9 8 6 5
              ◇ 10 4 2
              ♣ A K
```

FURTHER ANALYSIS

The end game was reduced to a curious guess. If the defenders were good, it was necessary to play for a specific holding. If they were bad, I could play for a mistake. Was East's diamond discard good or accidental?

41

Hand 9

BOTH VULNERABLE
EAST DEALS

South
♠ A K Q J 8 6 3 2
♡ J 10 5
◊ —
♣ K 7

This is a good hand. It's disappointing to hear East open ONE
DIAMOND. I can do a number of things with this. I can bid
four spades. I can double. Or, I can bid one spade and 'walk'
the hand. Who knows what's right? I don't. I guess DOUBLE.
West PASSES and Alex jumps to THREE CLUBS. East in turn
jumps to FIVE DIAMONDS and I still have eight solid spades
which I haven't bid. Not too late. I intend to bid them now.
The question is how many spades to bid. I don't expect West
to find a heart lead and there's no reason to think that will
automatically be fatal anyway. I'm bidding SIX SPADES. I
may go down. I may make it. Seven may be cold. And they
may save. Three good things can happen. Only one bad thing
can happen.

BOTH VULNERABLE
EAST DEALS

♠ 10 9 7
♡ A 4 2
◊ J 9
♣ A 10 8 6 2

```
   N
 W   E
   S
```

♠ A K Q J 8 6 3 2
♡ J 10 5
◊ —
♣ K 7

West	North	East	South
		1 ◊	Double
Pass	3 ♣	5 ◊	6 ♠
Pass	Pass	Pass	

LEAD: ◊ 2

West leads the two of diamonds and Alex puts down an excellent dummy. Good enough that seven is possible although not likely. I ruff East's ace of diamonds and play the spade ace. These are one-one.

Time to start clubs. I play the king and seven. West plays the jack on the second round and East who played the three now discards a diamond.

Not good.

I had hoped to set up a club trick for a heart discard. Now I'm going to have to set up a heart trick and that's not going to be easy. I suspect East has the king and queen of hearts although he may have only one of them.

I ruff dummy's last diamond in my hand.

If West shows out, it would leave East with ten diamonds plus one of each. I would be cold by leading the jack of hearts. East would win with a singleton honor and be endplayed or West would cover and I would duck, leaving West endplayed in two suits.

As it is, West follows with the seven. This means East has seven or eight diamonds, one spade, one club, and either three or four hearts.

In this case, I can not set up a heart trick but I can endplay East if he has both heart honors.

I lead the jack of hearts hoping West will err and cover if he does have an honor. He doesn't cover and East wins with the king. He returns the nine of hearts. I play the ten which wins so I am home.

COMPLETE HAND

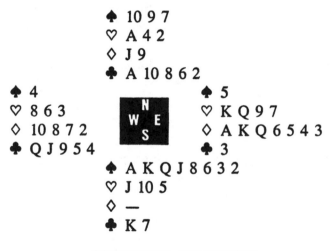

```
                  ♠ 10 9 7
                  ♡ A 4 2
                  ◇ J 9
                  ♣ A 10 8 6 2
    ♠ 4                        ♠ 5
    ♡ 8 6 3          N         ♡ K Q 9 7
    ◇ 10 8 7 2    W     E      ◇ A K Q 6 5 4 3
    ♣ Q J 9 5 4      S         ♣ 3
                  ♠ A K Q J 8 6 3 2
                  ♡ J 10 5
                  ◇ —
                  ♣ K 7
```

FURTHER ANALYSIS

If, when I cashed the king of clubs and led the seven, and West played low, it would be reasonable to finesse the ten of clubs. This would insure the contract at a cost of an overtrick when clubs are three-three. Six spades is an excellent contract and is worth making.

Hand 10

NORTH/SOUTH VULNERABLE
EAST DEALS

South
♠ A K 6 5 4
♡ 8 6 3
◇ A K
♣ J 10 5

I open ONE SPADE in second seat and Alex makes a limit raise of THREE SPADES. I have a sound opener and I continue to FOUR SPADES. West leads the four of hearts and we're in trouble already.

NORTH/SOUTH VULNERABLE
EAST DEALS

♠ Q 10 8 3 2
♡ K 5
◇ 8 6 4
♣ A 4 2

```
    N
 W     E
    S
```

♠ A K 6 5 4
♡ 9 6 3
◇ A K
♣ J 10 5

West	North	East	South
		Pass	1♠
Pass	3♠	Pass	4♠
Pass	Pass	Pass	

LEAD: ♡4

45

The heart lead is an extremely bad sign because against a suit contract, defenders don't (or shouldn't) underlead aces. These defenders are good so I know we are starting with two fast heart losers. This means I'll have to negotiate a now familiar club combination for one loser if I am to succeed.

I play low from dummy at trick one and East takes the jack and the ace. West, who led the four, followed with the two marking him with Q10x42. East switches to the diamond ten and I win the ace.

I draw trump in two rounds, West having the nine and East the jack-seven. West pitches the eight of hearts so I have a perfect count of this suit. Next the king of diamonds followed by a heart ruff and a diamond ruff in my hand. East plays the queen on this trick so I can add that to my store of information.

WHAT DO I KNOW?

The cards I know for sure are these.

West	East
♠ 9	♠ J 7
♡ Q 10 8 4 2	♡ A J 7
◊ 5 3 2 (?)	◊ Q 10 9 (?)
♣ ?	♣ ?

I have to guess the clubs and act appropriately if possible. If I think either opponent has both the king and queen of clubs, I can endplay him by leading the jack.

Can the club honors be in one hand? Let's see. If East has them both, that would give him approximately,

♠ J 7
♡ A J 7
◊ Q 10 9 x
♣ K Q x x

46

This looks like an opening bid to me. Since East passed as dealer, I don't think he has both club honors.

Can West have them? If so, he would have something like:

♠ 9
♡ Q 10 8 4 2
◇ J 5 3 2
♣ K Q 8

I would expect him to lead the club king instead of the four of hearts.

I'm sure the club honors are divided. The clues and inferences used here are quite strong ones. Not nebulous as on other occasions.

If the club honors are divided, I can't get a second trick by force unless someone has a doubleton honor and I can figure out who it is.

On the basis of the evidence, West is more likely to have the doubleton honor if one exists, but it is possible for East to have it. Nothing has been proven one way or another.

One fact does stand out. I can't make four spades if there is no doubleton club honor out. Therefore, I must make the assumption that it exists.

Shall I play East or West for the doubleton?

Strangely, it doesn't matter. Because I am playing in a trump contract and because I have been able to eliminate all suits and still have a trump in both hands, I can executive an endplay on either opponent.

I cash the club ace and lead another. West wins with the queen and thinks. This is promising. Sure enough, he has no more clubs and his diamond lead gives me a sluff and a ruff.

COMPLETE HAND

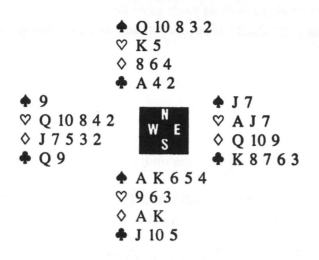

```
                ♠ Q 10 8 3 2
                ♡ K 5
                ◇ 8 6 4
                ♣ A 4 2
♠ 9                              ♠ J 7
♡ Q 10 8 4 2         N           ♡ A J 7
◇ J 7 5 3 2      W       E       ◇ Q 10 9
♣ Q 9                S           ♣ K 8 7 6 3
                ♠ A K 6 5 4
                ♡ 9 6 3
                ◇ A K
                ♣ J 10 5
```

FURTHER ANALYSIS

First, in the bidding, Alex did well to make a limit raise rather than to jump to four spades on the basis of having five trump.

In the play, the winning line was easily found when it was clear that the club honors couldn't be in the same hand. Ace and another club would endplay EITHER opponent if he started with a doubleton honor. It wasn't necessary to guess who had it.

Note the importance of the ten in the above club combination. Compare these two positions.

```
                A 4 2
Q 9 8 6 3                   K 7
                J 10 5
```

In this position, ace and another endplays East. There is nothing he can do about it.

```
                A 4 2
Q 10 9 7 3                          K 7
                J 8 5
```

In this position, East can play the king under the ace and West's
Q10 will be two tricks.

```
                A 4 2
Q 7                          K 10 9 6 3
                J 8 5
```

In this position, West is the victim, and this time he can't escape
the endplay.

Hand 11

EAST/WEST VULNERABLE
WEST DEALS

South
♠ J 10 5
♡ 7 2
◊ A K Q 10 9 7 6 5
♣ —

West opens ONE HEART and East responds ONE SPADE. I have another tactical decision. I can bid from two to five diamonds or I suppose I could pass.

I decide the vulnerability is right so I go for the throat with FIVE DIAMONDS. They may not have a game but I'm willing to believe they do. Unless I'm very, very unlucky, I should be down three at worst.

West DOUBLES to end the auction.

West leads the king of clubs. If that's the best thing he has to lead, it means some of the other points in the majors may be in Alex's hand.

EAST/WEST VULNERABLE
WEST DEALS

```
            ♠ A 4 2
            ♡ A Q 6 5 4
            ◊ 2
            ♣ 8 6 5 3

                  N
               W     E
                  S

            ♠ J 10 5
            ♡ 7 2
            ◊ A K Q 10 9 7 6 5
            ♣ —
```

West	North	East	South
1 ♡	Pass	1 ♠	5 ◊
Double	Pass	Pass	Pass

LEAD: ♣K

Thank you, Alex. Unless diamonds are four-zero, this is cold and I have chances for an overtrick.

I ruff the club and draw trump in two rounds, West having the doubleton jack. I've got to throw something from dummy, it could be right to run off more trump but since I'm not sure what to pitch from dummy, I will hold the trumps for the time being.

If I wish to, I can guarantee making five diamonds doubled by taking a safety play in hearts. I can play the ace of hearts which protects against a singleton king in East's hand. Then, assuming nothing happens, I will ruff a club and lead my second heart toward the queen.

This will lose only if East has Kx of hearts giving West Jxxx.

This is inconsistent with this pair's bidding methods so I can assume the safety play will work.

Should I do this? I think not. Five diamonds doubled is a likely contract so if I have a good chance for an overtrick I'll take it if it doesn't jeapordize my contract.

There is a good play for an overtrick which depends on West having the king of hearts (almost certain) and one spade honor (very likely). What after all, does West have to open the bidding, to say nothing of the double?

At trick four I lead the jack of spades. If West covers I will have to decide if West has the KQ alone or if East has the missing honor.

In fact, West plays low and East wins the queen. Back comes a club which I ruff. I intend to try to squeeze West out of his spade honor (hopefully) and his hearts (still assuming he has the king). In preparation for this, I lead the spade four to the ace getting nothing useful and ruff dummy's last club back to my hand. Now the rest of the diamonds. West eventually throws the king of spades so I score my ten and then take a heart finesse for the overtrick. I see from the actual hand that there was no defense as long as I guessed spades.

COMPLETE HAND

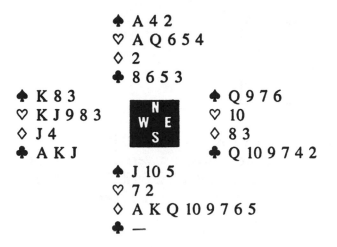

♠ A 4 2
♡ A Q 6 5 4
◊ 2
♣ 8 6 5 3

♠ K 8 3
♡ K J 9 8 3
◊ J 4
♣ A K J

♠ Q 9 7 6
♡ 10
◊ 8 3
♣ Q 10 9 7 4 2

♠ J 10 5
♡ 7 2
◊ A K Q 10 9 7 6 5
♣ —

FURTHER ANALYSIS

Turns out they can't make a thing.

Chapter 2

A 4		Q 10
Q 10	OR	A 4

This combination is a bit of an odd ball in that you will never get a second trick (well, maybe never) unless the opponents lead it for you and you can capitalize on it. There are, however, many tactical considerations which will be pertinent to the REST of the hand.

Hand 12

BOTH VULNERABLE
SOUTH DEALS

South
♠ A 4
♥ A J 9 5 3
♦ A 9 4
♣ A Q 8

I open ONE HEART and Alex finds a raise to THREE HEARTS. Opposite a limit raise I should have a good chance of slam. Seven might be cold but I don't care to explore when success is unlikely. Better I think to bid SIX HEARTS and give West an uninformed choices of leads.

He chooses the ten of clubs.

BOTH VULNERABLE
SOUTH DEALS

♠ Q 10
♡ Q 8 7 6 2
◇ K J 2
♣ K J 4

```
    N
  W   E
    S
```

♠ A 4
♡ A J 9 5 3
◇ A 9 4
♣ A Q 8

West	North	East	South
			1 ♡
Pass	3 ♡	Pass	6 ♡
Pass	Pass	Pass	

LEAD: ♣ 10

In spite of a ten-card fit and lots of points, this is not a good slam. Fair maybe, but not good. Our bidding is not at fault though. The real villian is the matching duplication which could not be judged in the auction.

I win the club ten with dummy's jack and lead the queen of hearts. This is necessary to cater to K104 in East's hand.

East covers and I win the ace. Caution was wise because West does show out pitching the club six. In spite of the danger of a club ruff, I reenter dummy with the king of clubs. This risk is necessary because the spades and diamonds, in total, offer a position I want to keep intact. The club wins so I can draw trump with no further problems. When I cash the ace of clubs, the position becomes:

♠ Q 10
♡ 7 2
◇ K J 2
♣ —

♠ A 4
♡ 5 3
◇ A 9 4
♣ —

I can finesse the jack of diamonds, which is easily the worst of my available plays. This is about fifty percent.

I can cash the ace and king of diamonds hoping to drop the queen. If this fails, I can exit with the jack. Whoever wins will have to lead a spade which gives me a trick half the time. Call this line fifty-seven percent, give or take.

The third line is closer to ninety percent.

I cash the ace of spades and exit with the four. If East wins, I am home because he has to lead a diamond or else give me a sluff and a ruff. East will have the king of spades exactly half the time.

If West wins the spade, he will have to lead a diamond. There are four relevant positions and three of them are good for me.

```
              K J 2
   Q 10 x                 x x x
              A 9 4
```

West has both the queen and ten of diamonds. I will lose no diamonds.

```
            K J 2
Q x x                      10 x x
            A 9 4
```

West has the queen, East the ten. I play the two when West leads the suit, East plays the ten and I win. I finesse the jack, and once again, no diamond losers.

```
            K J 2
10 x x                     Q x x
            A 9 4
```

West has the ten, East the queen. When West leads a diamond, I duck and East has no winning play. In spite of the diamond queen being offside, it doesn't matter. No diamond losers.

```
            K J 2
x x x                      Q 10 x
            A 9 4
```

East has both diamond honors. This is the only bad holding for me. And note it is only bad if *WEST* wins the spade. If East wins it, his Q10x of diamonds won't help at all.

The line of ace and a spade wins:
50% when East wins the king, plus 75% of the other 50% when West wins the king. Total = 87½%.

In practice, West wins the spade and he leads a diamond as he had to. When I play dummy's two, East plays the queen, so there are no further anxieties.

COMPLETE HAND

```
               ♠ Q 10
               ♡ Q 8 7 6 2
               ◇ K J 2
               ♣ K J 4
♠ K 8 6 2                          ♠ J 9 7 5 3
♡ —            ┌─────────┐         ♡ K 10 4
◇ 10 8 7 3     │    N    │         ◇ Q 6 5
♣ 10 9 7 6 2   │  W   E  │         ♣ 5 3
               │    S    │
               └─────────┘
               ♠ A 4
               ♡ A J 9 5 3
               ◇ A 9 4
               ♣ A Q 8
```

Hand 13

NORTH/SOUTH VULNERABLE
WEST DEALS

South
♠ A 7
♡ J 8 2
◇ A Q J 8 6 4
♣ K 3

West and North PASS and East opens ONE CLUB. I have a good hand but I can't see anything except ONE DIAMOND. West PASSES again and Alex raises to TWO DIAMONDS. Maybe I'm being a little optimistic but I'm going to take a shot at THREE NOTRUMP.

West must not have heard his partner's opening bid because he leads the five of spades. Probably the last thing I wanted to see.

NORTH/SOUTH VULNERABLE
WEST DEALS

```
           ♠ Q 10
           ♡ A 6 5 4
           ◇ 10 9 3
           ♣ A 5 4 2

              N
           W     E
              S

           ♠ A 7
           ♡ J 8 2
           ◇ A Q J 8 6 4
           ♣ K 3
```

West	North	East	South
Pass	Pass	1♣	1◇
Pass	2◇	Pass	3NT
Pass	Pass	Pass	

LEAD: ♠5

Right. The only lead that gives me a problem. My first in-clination is to play the ten, hoping the opening bidder has the king and not the jack. But since first impressions are only good in bars, I'm going to take a second look.

If the diamond finesse wins, I will make this regardless of how I play the spades. Only if the diamond finesse loses will my spade guess be crucial to the contract.

Assuming the worst case, that the diamond finesse loses, what does that tell me about the spades?

It tells me that West can't have the king of spades. The auc-tion marks West with at least five spades and if he had both kings, he would have bid over my one diamond bid.

I play dummy's ten on the theory that this gives me the best chance to make three notrump. If East has the king and jack, it makes no difference. It does make a difference if West has the king of diamonds and the jack of spades.

East plays the king so I've doing the right thing so far. I go to the ace of clubs and take the diamond finesse losing to the king. Another spade gives me no option but to cash out which I do. Ten tricks.

COMPLETE HAND

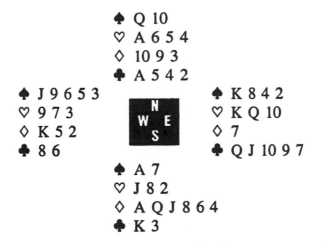

♠ Q 10
♡ A 6 5 4
◊ 10 9 3
♣ A 5 4 2

♠ J 9 6 5 3
♡ 9 7 3
◊ K 5 2
♣ 8 6

♠ K 8 4 2
♡ K Q 10
◊ 7
♣ Q J 10 9 7

♠ A 7
♡ J 8 2
◊ A Q J 8 6 4
♣ K 3

FURTHER ANALYSIS

Whenever you play a contract which is cold against all but one occurrence, you should ask yourself,

"If the one bad thing occurs, how will that affect the rest of the hand?"

Doing this on the above hand led you to say,

"If West has the king of diamonds, he can't have the king of spades. Therefore, play him for the jack."

Say these were the two hands.

♠ Q 9
♡ A 6 5 4
◊ 10 9 3
♣ A 5 4 2

♠ A 7
♡ J 8 2
◊ A Q J 8 6 4
♣ K 3

SAME BIDDING

West	North	East	South
Pass	Pass	1♣	1◊
Pass	2◊	Pass	3NT
Pass	Pass	Pass	

West leads the four of spades.

On the same basis as when dummy had the Q10, you should say,

"West can't have the spade *AND* diamond kings. If West has the king of diamonds, East has the king of spades. Play dummy's nine of spades and hope West has led from J10xxx."

This play could cost you an overtrick, but it could gain you the contract. I admit the extra trick could cost you at matchpoints, but at IMPs, I would certainly make the play.

First impressions aren't always wrong!

Hand 14

NO ONE VULNERABLE
NORTH DEALS

South
♠ A 5
♡ K J 10 7 6 4
◊ A 6 5
♣ K 9

I have a routine ONE HEART in third seat and Alex responds with a Drury TWO CLUBS. We play that this promises trump support in contrast to a Drury version which might not promise support. I have a hand which should make game viable so I bid it without wasting time, FOUR HEARTS. West leads the queen of diamonds and Alex puts down a nice hand.

NO ONE VULNERABLE
NORTH DEALS

　　　　♠ Q 10
　　　　♡ A 9 8 5
　　　　◊ K 9 2
　　　　♣ Q 8 6 3

　　　　　N
　　　W　　E
　　　　　S

　　　　♠ A 5
　　　　♡ K J 10 7 6 4
　　　　◊ A 6 5
　　　　♣ K 9

West	North	East	South
	Pass	Pass	1♡
Pass	2♣ (a)	Pass	4♡
Pass	Pass	Pass	

(a) Drury

LEAD: ◊ Q

Alex has a fine hand for his Drury call although I am probably biased by the fact that four hearts is a good contract. I do think Drury was a good bid. Three hearts, which was the alternative, would have gotten us dangerously high if I had, say, no ace of spades and one less heart.

I win the diamond lead in my hand and play the king and ace of hearts. If anyone has a void in hearts, I would guess it to be East. This is because if someone had a void, they would try to bid. On our auction West would have had an easier time bidding than East so I assume West doesn't have the void. I estimate this rationale as very inconsequential so I'm not spending a lot of time on it.

Hearts are singleton queen with West and two small with East. With trumps divided, I am cold for four hearts and can try for an overtrick.

One chance is to establish a second club trick. I can get two club tricks if East has the singleton, doubleton, or tripleton ace of clubs. I will lead to the king and then duck a club on the way back. If East has three or fewer clubs, I will be able to set up dummy's queen.

Also, if either opponent has jack ten doubleton or third, I can get a second club trick.

When I lead a club, West takes my king with the ace and returns the ten of diamonds to dummy's king. It's still possible for the jack ten of clubs to fall, but when I play queen and a club ruff, West drops the ten, but still no jack. I can't get a second club trick, but there is still the chance for an endplay. I enter dummy with the nine of hearts and ruff the last club, East having the jack.

I have two choices for an endplay. I can play a diamond to West and hope to guess on his spade return, or I can play ace and a spade and hope whoever wins has no more diamonds.

I know West has the jack of diamonds, so for the ace and a spade play to work, East must have the spade king and no diamonds. East's diamonds so far have been the three and the four. No promises, but this suggests East has three diamonds.

I judge the chances that East has two diamonds and the king of spades as less than my chances of guessing spades when West leads them. As he does. When I lead my diamond, West wins and leads the seven of spades. I note East follows on the diamond so the other line would have failed.

How shall I guess the spades?

As usual, a reconstruction of the opponents' hands may help. East hasn't shown much yet, but West has shown quite a bit.

He has:

♠ x x x x x
♡ Q
◇ Q J 10 (x)
♣ A 10 x

West has five spades and might have six. I think West would have bid one spade with the king so I'm guessing East has that card. Perforce I play dummy's ten and that forces the king. Making five.

COMPLETE HAND

♠ Q 10
♡ A 9 8 5
◇ K 9 2
♣ Q 8 6 3

♠ J 7 4 3 2   ♠ K 9 8 6
♡ Q   ♡ 3 2
◇ Q J 10 8   ◇ 7 4 3
♣ A 10 7   ♣ J 5 4 2

♠ A 5
♡ K J 10 7 6 4
◇ A 6 5
♣ K 9

FURTHER ANALYSIS

The club combination had to be started from dummy in case East had three or fewer clubs with the ace. Leading the king from hand gives up on these combinations.

Hand 15

NO ONE VULNERABLE
EAST DEALS

South
♠ K Q J 9 7
♡ A Q 5 2
◇ A 4
♣ 8 3

When East announces a skip bid, I know this hand will be awkward. East follows his warning with THREE DIAMONDS. I can well use my ten seconds to choose my bid and I opt for DOUBLE. West PASSES and Alex bids FOUR DIAMONDS. Since he could be under pressure I bid only FOUR SPADES but I feel I still haven't done full justice to the hand. Alex has extras too because he raises to FIVE SPADES. This clearly emphasizes diamonds and asks me to bid six spades with a diamond control. Since I have a very good hand I cue bid SIX DIAMONDS in case Alex wants to bid seven. Alex bids only SIX SPADES, but I can tell he was thinking of bidding more. I have to PASS and West leads the queen of clubs.

NO ONE VULNERABLE
EAST DEALS

```
              ♠ A 8 6 2
              ♡ K J 10 6
              ◊ Q 10
              ♣ A K 5

                  N
               W     E
                  S

              ♠ K Q J 9 7
              ♡ A Q 5 2
              ◊ A 4
              ♣ 8 3
```

West	North	East	South
		3 ◊	Double
Pass	4 ◊	Pass	4 ♠
Pass	5 ♣	Pass	6 ◊
Pass	6 ♠	Pass	Pass
Pass			

LEAD: ♣Q

Wrong contract. Seven hearts is cold. Don't know how to bid it though. What is clear is that anyone in six hearts will make seven so I should try to make seven spades if possible.

There are two slight possibilities. West can have a singleton king of diamonds or six clubs plus the king of diamonds doubleton. In this case I can squeeze West in the minors.

Or, West can have the singleton jack of diamonds or six clubs plus the doubleton jack of diamonds. In this case, I lead the queen of diamonds which East will cover and then squeeze West in the minors.

I expect the second scenario to be more likely than the first so I follow the described line. I win the club ace, draw two rounds of trump, which divide two-two, and lead the queen of diamonds. East covers and I win. Seven tricks later, I lead my last spade in this hoped for position.

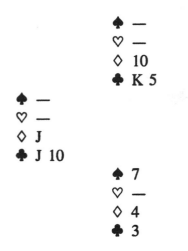

```
                    ♠ —
                    ♡ —
                    ◇ 10
                    ♣ K 5
         ♠ —
         ♡ —
         ◇ J
         ♣ J 10
                    ♠ 7
                    ♡ —
                    ◇ 4
                    ♣ 3
```

West concedes showing that he did have the jack of diamonds along with seven clubs.

COMPLETE HAND

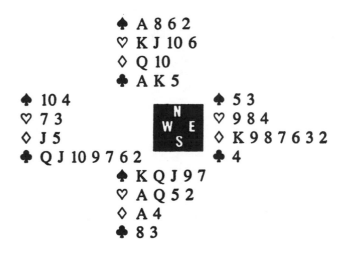

```
                    ♠ A 8 6 2
                    ♡ K J 10 6
                    ◇ Q 10
                    ♣ A K 5
   ♠ 10 4                         ♠ 5 3
   ♡ 7 3              N           ♡ 9 8 4
   ◇ J 5           W   E          ◇ K 9 8 7 6 3 2
   ♣ Q J 10 9 7 6 2   S           ♣ 4
                    ♠ K Q J 9 7
                    ♡ A Q 5 2
                    ◇ A 4
                    ♣ 8 3
```

A lot of work to get up to average. There's a cute falsecard available. Say the hands were:

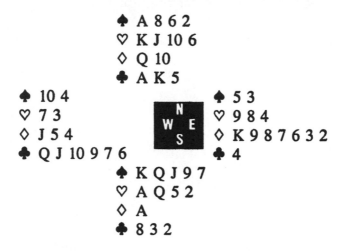

```
              ♠ A 8 6 2
              ♥ K J 10 6
              ◊ Q 10
              ♣ A K 5
♠ 10 4                        ♠ 5 3
♥ 7 3              N          ♥ 9 8 4
◊ J 5 4          W   E        ◊ K 9 8 7 6 3 2
♣ Q J 10 9 7 6     S          ♣ 4
              ♠ K Q J 9 7
              ♥ A Q 5 2
              ◊ A
              ♣ 8 3 2
```

South can lead the queen of diamonds and East will have to cover (or he will think he does) and the squeeze will work again.

Hand 16

NORTH/SOUTH VULNERABLE
NORTH DEALS

South
♠ Q 10 2
♡ A 4
◊ K Q 10 3
♣ A K Q J

When I hold a hand this good I expect to be able to open it and sure enough there are two PASSES to me in third seat. I open TWO NOTRUMP showing 20 to 22. Alex futzes around and comes up with a raise to FOUR NOTRUMP. Should I accept it or let it go?

This is marginal because my values are only slightly on the heavy side of my promised range. Influenced by the ten of spades, I accept the offer and try SIX NOTRUMP. West leads the nine of clubs so I won't be having any help on the opening lead.

NORTH/SOUTH VULNERABLE
NORTH DEALS

♠ K J 4
♥ Q 10
♦ A 9 8 5
♣ 10 6 5 4

```
    N
  W   E
    S
```

♠ Q 10 2
♥ A 4
♦ K Q 10 3
♣ A K Q J

West	North	East	South
	Pass	Pass	2NT
Pass	4NT	Pass	6NT
Pass	Pass	Pass	

LEAD: ♣9

Hopeless. I wonder who bid too much. I'm sure Alex will tell me if I ask.

In the meantime, I am in a terrible contract but I'm going to try to look enthusiastic about it until the verdict is in. I thank Alex and settle down to looking for a twelfth trick.

There are two or three possible lines. None very good, I can

1. Hope for a stiff king of hearts. Unrealistic.
2. I can run off all my minors and lead a spade. If someone has the stiff ace, he may be endplayed in hearts. Also unrealistic.

3. I can lead dummy's queen of hearts and hope West has the singleton jack. This is the most unrealistic of all of these. Perhaps, if I lead the queen, East will fail to cover.

4. I can try to sneak one round of spades by the opponents. If someone started with doubleton ace of spades, I can try to endplay them later. This is, under the circumstances, the best line so far.

5. At the risk of going down two extra tricks, I can try to sneak a heart through at trick two by leading low to the queen. My guess is that this play will work about ten percent of the time.

Why would this play work at all? The reason that it could work is that West will not know what is actually happening. He will be laboring under an illusion. You hope West thinks the hand is like this.

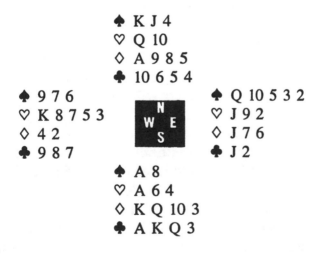

```
                    ♠ K J 4
                    ♡ Q 10
                    ◇ A 9 8 5
                    ♣ 10 6 5 4
      ♠ 9 7 6                        ♠ Q 10 5 3 2
      ♡ K 8 7 5 3         N          ♡ J 9 2
      ◇ 4 2            W      E       ◇ J 7 6
      ♣ 9 8 7             S          ♣ J 2
                    ♠ A 8
                    ♡ A 6 4
                    ◇ K Q 10 3
                    ♣ A K Q 3
```

From West's point of view, declarer would lead a heart to the Q10 and try to guess them. Failing this, declarer would fall back on the spade finesse. In the above layout, West would concede the contract if he took his heart king because that would give declarer twelve tricks. If West ducks and is able to do so smoothly, declarer may play the ten. This loses to the jack and declarer's chances are over.

In the real hand, with Q10 opposite A4, the heart play has a chance of working because West won't know what is happening. Remember, he will have to make a fast decision or else he will give away the situation. Believe me, a defender can do the wrong thing.

Now, the question is, should I try this strange play, risking down three if they set up hearts, or should I just go down one?

This is a tough question. As I said, I think the swindle will work about ten percent of the time. If West has the heart king, he won't duck if he also has the ace of spades. He will cash out and beat me. And, if he has the king and jack of hearts he won't duck because he will see that I'm going to get two tricks regardless of what I do. The chance that West has the king of hearts is fifty percent. The chances that East has both the spade ace and the heart jack is twenty-five percent. In combination, there is a twelve-and-a-half percent chance that West has just the heart king. I expect a good defender will duck more times than not, hence my estimate of ten percent. The second question is whether it is right to try this. I think so because on many occasions, the defenders will take the king of hearts but they won't know to return one. They may be so happy to beat six notrump that they just bang down the ace of spades. Elation is a curious thing at the bridge table. It's wonderful to experience it, but it's hard to think clearly while under its influence.

I vote for the swindle and try it. At trick two I lead the heart four. West is caught off guard and he starts to think. I wish he'd think faster because once he realizes he's given the show away, he will probably take his king. He does take it and I'm faced with three down if they lead a heart back. East has ideas of his own and on his turn to play, he follows with an emphatic jack of hearts. He wants, or thinks he wants, a spade lead. West agrees and leads one, so I escape for down one after all.

COMPLETE HAND

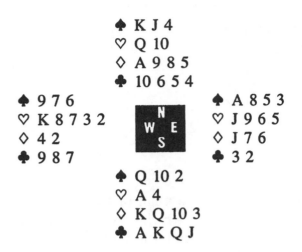

```
              ♠ K J 4
              ♡ Q 10
              ◊ A 9 8 5
              ♣ 10 6 5 4
♠ 9 7 6                        ♠ A 8 5 3
♡ K 8 7 3 2      N             ♡ J 9 6 5
◊ 4 2         W     E          ◊ J 7 6
♣ 9 8 7          S             ♣ 3 2
              ♠ Q 10 2
              ♡ A 4
              ◊ K Q 10 3
              ♣ A K Q J
```

FURTHER ANALYSIS

It was probably reasonable to try to make six notrump because going down rates to be very poor. Alex was a little bit exuberant in the auction, by his own admission.

I think I underrated one of the other plays. Leading the queen from dummy has real chances. East with, say, K752 might duck expecting me to have something like AJ98 or A984. Ducking could easily be right.

Hand 17

BOTH VULNERABLE
SOUTH DEALS

South
♠ K 4 3
♡ A K Q 8 6 2
♢ A K
♣ A 4

Another good hand worth an opening of TWO CLUBS. Alex responds TWO DIAMONDS, which only denies a good suit to show. He can have a good hand which will show itself later. I rebid TWO HEARTS and Alex raises to THREE HEARTS. This shows at least eight points and I'm willing to commit to a slam. I wonder if I can find out about seven.

♠ A x
♡ x x x x
♢ Q x x x
♣ x x x

This dummy makes seven hearts cold so it is clear that seven should be investigated.

I think if I cue bid FOUR DIAMONDS, I can keep the auction flexible. Alex cue bids FOUR SPADES so seven remains possible. Blackwood won't solve anything so I try another cue bid. FIVE CLUBS. Alex may be able to bid six clubs for me which would be nice. He doesn't. Instead he signs off in FIVE HEARTS. Now I can cue bid FIVE SPADES. Now Alex can cue bid the queen of diamonds if he has it. He has denied the king, so I think he would know to cue bid the queen. Alex bids SIX CLUBS which means I think, that he is cue bidding the queen of clubs.

Wrong queen, Alex. He may have the diamond queen, so I cue bid SIX DIAMONDS giving him one last chance which he declines. SIX HEARTS. This is the final contract and I play it with the ten of spades lead.

BOTH VULNERABLE
SOUTH DEALS

♠ A 8 2
♡ J 10 7 3
◊ 8 4 3 2
♣ Q 10

```
  N
W   E
  S
```

♠ K 4 3
♡ A K Q 8 6 2
◊ A K
♣ A 4

West	North	East	South
			2♣
Pass	2◊	Pass	2♡
Pass	3♡	Pass	4◊
Pass	4♠	Pass	5♣
Pass	5♡	Pass	5♠
Pass	6♣	Pass	6◊
Pass	6♡	Pass	Pass
Pass			

LEAD: ♠ 10

A typical Alex minimum. Hard to believe we made five grand slam tries and find six is not cold.

77

I have a spade loser and a club loser. I could try the four of clubs play as on the previous hand, but since I have an elimination that gives me almost an even money play, I will try for honesty rather than a swindle.

I win the king of spades and play the trump ace. When they divide, I cash the king noting West has the singleton. My intention is to eliminate the diamonds and to throw the opponents in with a spade. They will have to lead a club and I will have have to guess them.

I cash two diamonds, enter dummy with a heart and ruff a diamond. Back to dummy with the ace of spades, East dropping the jack, and ruff the last diamond. When I exit with a spade, West wins the nine, East following, and leads the three of clubs. If West has the king or jack of clubs, I am cold. I just have to guess which honor he holds.

Since East isn't looking confident, I assume he hasn't both club honors so that they are, in fact, guessable.

Which play is right? Do I have a clue or it is a guess? I think I have a one-hundred percent clue and I'm going to act on it. I play the ten and East concedes.

COMPLETE HAND

```
              ♠ A 8 2
              ♡ J 10 7 3
              ◇ 8 4 3 2
              ♣ Q 10
  ♠ 10 9 7              ♠ Q J 6 5
  ♡ 4          N        ♡ 9 5
  ◇ J 9 5    W   E      ◇ Q 10 7 6
  ♣ J 8 7 6 3 2  S      ♣ K 9 5
              ♠ K 4 3
              ♡ A K Q 8 6 2
              ◇ A K
              ♣ A 4
```

78

What was the giveaway that made the ten of clubs the correct play?

The clue is in what the defenders did. East could have won the third round of spades but did not. In fact, he went out of his way to avoid winning it. When I went to the ace of spades, East played his jack so that he wouldn't have to win the next spade.

From East's point of view, if he won the spade and led a club, I would have no choice but to play low. If West wins the spade and leads a club, declarer may go wrong. He shouldn't go wrong when East puts on his unblocking exhibition, but a chance is better than no chance. A nice play by East.

FURTHER ANALYSIS

The elimination wasn't a fifty percent play because some of the time, the clubs are unguessable. Assume the defense plays their spades correctly.If West (50%) has the club king, I am down when East wins the spade and leads a club. When East has the club king, I go down when he also has the jack.

Hand 18

NO ONE VULNERABLE
EAST DEALS

South
♠ Q 10
♡ Q 10
◊ A Q J 2
♣ K Q 10 5 3

East PASSES and I open ONE NOTRUMP. Any time I have a near balanced sixteen count I consider one notrump and compare it with the alternatives. If I don't open one notrump, I have to bid one club or one diamond. In either case, I won't like rebidding after a one heart or one spade response.

Alex responds TWO SPADES, asking for a minor suit. I bid THREE CLUBS, raised to SIX CLUBS.

West leads the eight of spades and I see I have some guesses to make.

NO ONE VULNERABLE
EAST DEALS

```
        ♠ A 4
        ♡ A 4
        ◊ K 10 6 5
        ♣ A 8 6 4 2

              N
          W       E
              S

        ♠ Q 10
        ♡ Q 10
        ◊ A Q J 2
        ♣ K Q 10 5 3
```

West	North	East	South
		Pass	1NT
Pass	2♣ (a)	Pass	3♣
Pass	6♣	Pass	Pass
Pass			

(a) Minor Suit

LEAD: ♠8

Too bad. If both of my major suit queens were one king, this would be cold. What should I do here? I have two clear lines.

1. I can duck the opening lead and hope West led from the king. In theory, this is even money although I doubt West would lead from a king into an opening notrump bidder.
2. Win the spade ace, draw trump, cash the diamonds, and exit with a spade. Whoever wins must lead a heart.

What are the percentages of each play?

The percent for play one, of ducking the opening lead can only be guessed. How likely is West to lead from the king of spades. I guess less than fifty percent. Say forty.

How about line two? It feels like a fifty-fifty proposition. Fortunately, the percentages can be broken down exactly.

If West wins the king of spades, he will have to lead a heart. That will be onside exactly half the time.

If East wins the king of spades, I will always succeed when East has the KJ of hearts and I will be down if West has the KJ of hearts. These chances are even money. If the king and jack of hearts are divided, I will have an even chance of guessing.

This all adds up to a fifty percent line as I thought. It is actually better than that because I may get some help from careless signaling or I may get a silly sluff and a ruff.

When I win the ace of spades, East signals with the nine. I draw four rounds of clubs and four rounds of diamonds and consider what I've seen. In this case not much. Both opponents throw innocuous spades and hearts. What I had hoped for was an emphatic heartfelt signal but it didn't come.

I exit with the spade queen and East wins meaning line one would have failed. When East accurately returns a small heart I have to guess what to do and I don't see that I have much to go on. I can see one small clue. East seems to have good spades and since he did not double two spades, the reason might be that he has decent hearts too, and did not want to talk West out of a better lead. This is a slim clue but it's the only one I have. Queen! It wins. Is there anything to my logic or was it just lucky? I'll take it.

COMPLETE HAND

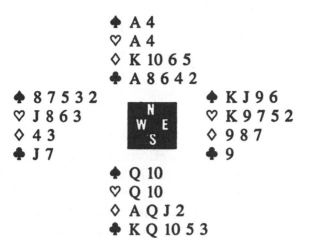

```
              ♠ A 4
              ♡ A 4
              ◇ K 10 6 5
              ♣ A 8 6 4 2
♠ 8 7 5 3 2                    ♠ K J 9 6
♡ J 8 6 3       N             ♡ K 9 7 5 2
◇ 4 3        W     E          ◇ 9 8 7
♣ J 7            S            ♣ 9
              ♠ Q 10
              ♡ Q 10
              ◇ A Q J 2
              ♣ K Q 10 5 3
```

FURTHER ANALYSIS

One comment in the bidding. Alex made a good practical bid when he bid six clubs. He could not really find that seven was cold if indeed it was, and his values weren't right for six notrump. Six clubs should have a play and he bid it.

In the play, this endplay has a better chance of working than on the previous hand because the defense has no options on who wins the spade. Here, the hand with the king has to win. The previous hand gave the defenders options so they had choices.

Chapter 3

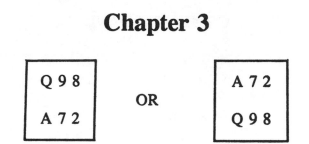

The usual problem with these two combinations is how to get two tricks. If left to your own efforts, you will usually lead toward the queen hoping the king is onside. This is not the only solution nor is getting a second trick the only problem. There are many variations within this suit and there are many defensive falsecards available when declarer plays this suit. It is one of the more exciting combinations to play.

Hand 19

EAST/WEST VULNERABLE
EAST DEALS

> *South*
> ♠ 7 5 2
> ♡ A 7 2
> ◊ K Q 8 5
> ♣ A K 3

East PASSES and I find myself with another good hand. Good hands are nice. You get to play more hands.

I open ONE NOTRUMP and Alex raises to THREE NOTRUMP.

West isn't too sure about his opening lead and he settles eventually on the jack of hearts.

Their convention card says the jack denies a higher honor so I know East has the heart king. Can I use this information. Perhaps.

84

EAST/WEST VULNERABLE
EAST DEALS

♠ K 3
♥ Q 9 8
♦ A J 10 4
♣ Q 7 6 4

```
      N
   W     E
      S
```

♠ 7 5 2
♥ A 7 2
♦ K Q 8 5
♣ A K 3

West	North	East	South
		Pass	1NT
Pass	3NT	Pass	Pass
Pass			

LEAD: ♥ J

This is a good lead for me because it assures me of nine tricks even if clubs don't divide. I have four diamonds, three clubs, and by covering the heart, I can set up a sure two tricks in hearts.

Before covering the heart jack I consider that the spade suit is spectacularly dangerous. If West leads a spade, the defense will get anywhere from three to six spade tricks if the ace is offside. Definitely in my interest to keep West off lead if possible.

If I cover the heart jack, I can set up a second heart, but West may use this entry to switch to a spade. Is it possible to keep West off play and still get nine tricks?

If I trust the lead to be from J10 or J10x, I think I can do it.

85

I do not cover the jack. Instead I let the jack come to my ace. I return a heart and finesse dummy's nine. If West has made an honest lead, this will force the king and I will have a ninth trick without letting West in. Of course, if West made an inspired lead from Jx and East has K10xxx, I'm going down.

Weighing the dangers I think it pretty clear to play this way. It is very possible for the spade ace to be offside and it is close to being guaranteed, I guess 95%, that West has the ten of hearts.

This play turns out successfully and East wins the heart king and clears the suit. I have now seen West play the J, 6 and ten of hearts, and East play the 5, K, and three. I believe East has the last heart, the four, because the correct lead from J1064 is probably the four. I can cash nine tricks now and hope for a tenth trick from clubs or spades. I'd like to try both and I think I can if I'm careful. If I cash diamonds first and then try clubs, I'll be in the dummy. I'd prefer to end in my hand to lead a spade. Certainly I'm not leading spades until I have nine tricks in.

To do this, I cash the clubs first. They don't divide and West has the four. Now four rounds of diamonds ending in my hand to lead a spade. No good, East claims.

At least the heart suit was successful and necessary.

COMPLETE HAND

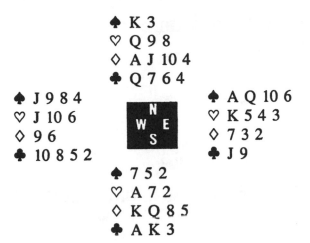

```
            ♠ K 3
            ♡ Q 9 8
            ◇ A J 10 4
            ♣ Q 7 6 4
♠ J 9 8 4                    ♠ A Q 10 6
♡ J 10 6        N           ♡ K 5 4 3
◇ 9 6        W   E          ◇ 7 3 2
♣ 10 8 5 2      S           ♣ J 9
            ♠ 7 5 2
            ♡ A 7 2
            ◇ K Q 8 5
            ♣ A K 3
```

FURTHER ANALYSIS

If, on the run of the diamonds, either opponent had thrown away the thirteenth heart, that would have guaranteed no ace of spades. Defenders with aces keep winners, not losers.

Hand 20

NORTH/SOUTH VULNERABLE
EAST DEALS

> *South*
> ♠ A 7 2
> ♡ 10 3
> ◊ K 10 4
> ♣ J 10 8 6 3

After three PASSES, Alex opens ONE HEART in fourth seat. East overcalls ONE SPADE and I choose ONE NOTRUMP. I have the values to bid and no sensible alternative to one notrump. I wish I had the ten or nine of spades.

Alex raises to THREE NOTRUMP which is passed out. West leads the ten of spades.

NORTH/SOUTH VULNERABLE
EAST DEALS

```
        ♠ Q 9 8
        ♡ K Q J 9 5
        ◊ Q J 3
        ♣ A K
```

```
          N
        W   E
          S
```

```
        ♠ A 7 2
        ♡ 10 3
        ◊ K 10 4
        ♣ J 10 8 6 3
```

West	North	East	South
		Pass	Pass
Pass	1 ♡	1 ♠	1NT
Pass	3NT	Pass	Pass
Pass			

LEAD: ♠ 10

This time I can think of no reason not to cover the ten of spades so I do so firmly. East plays the king and mentions some Duke he knows.

Should I take this? It's pretty clear that East has five or six spades to the KJ and one, but not both, of the missing aces. If he had both aces, he would have opened, and with none, he would not have overcalled.

If I take the spade, I will lead hearts. This will establish four hearts, two spades if the defense continues them, two clubs, and two diamonds, but only if I have time to get them.

The danger is that West will have the ace of hearts and can lead another spade. When East gets in with the ace of diamonds his spades will be good for down one.

Should I lead a diamond before the heart? Perhaps. But if West has the diamond ace and East the heart ace, I go down again.

Can I tell which ace to knock out?

No, but it isn't necessary. I have a counter to anything the defense can do.

It is?

Duck the first spade. If East continues, I finesse it to dummy's nine. Now if I guess wrong and West gets in first, he doesn't have a spade to lead. When East gets in later, his spades aren't good. I will have time to enjoy all my tricks before they enjoy theirs. Ten tricks.

COMPLETE HAND

```
              ♠ Q 9 8
              ♡ K Q J 9 5
              ◊ Q J 3
              ♣ A K
  ♠ 10 5                      ♠ K J 6 4 3
  ♡ A 7 6 4        N          ♡ 8 2
  ◊ 7 5 2       W   E         ◊ A 9 8 6
  ♣ Q 7 5 4        S          ♣ 9 2
              ♠ A 7 2
              ♡ 10 3
              ◊ K 10 4
              ♣ J 10 8 6 3
```

90

FURTHER ANALYSIS

East clearly misdefended. If he ducks the queen of spades at trick one, I will go down if I lead hearts. West will win and continue spades. East's ace of diamonds gets him in soon enough to cash out.

If I guess to lead diamonds first, I can make three notrump against any defense but that's not as good or as easy as a sure thing.

Remember East's problem. He could see the Q98 of spades so he knew his partner had 10x and not 109x.

Hand 21

NO ONE VULNERABLE
WEST DEALS

South
♠ K Q
♡ K Q 10 9 7 6 2
◊ Q 9 8
♣ A

West announces a skip bid and calls TWO DIAMONDS. This is passed to me and before acting, I ascertain it is a weak two. This seems obvious but I'd certainly hate to bid some number of hearts and discover it was FLANNERY showing, four spades and five hearts.

This would be a difficult hand to bid without our agreement. We have the understanding that reopening jumps are intermediate so I am comfortable bidding THREE HEARTS. Alex finds FOUR HEARTS which finishes the bidding.

NO ONE VULNERABLE
WEST DEALS

- ♠ 9 7 3
- ♡ J 8
- ◊ A 7 2
- ♣ Q J 10 4 2

```
    N
 W     E
    S
```

- ♠ K Q
- ♡ K Q 10 9 7 6 2
- ◊ Q 9 8
- ♣ A

LEAD: ◊ J

West thinks if they are good enough to bid, they are good enough to lead. He leads the jack of diamonds. This opponent's card implies standard leads so West can have the king of diamonds.

I play low from dummy prepared to win with my queen. It is a distinct disappointment to see East take the king with a muffled sigh of relief. If I've ever seen someone win a singleton king, this is the time.

Somewhat faster, I hope, than it takes me to write about it, I play the queen on the king. If I haven't done it smoothly, West will, or should, work out to give East a diamond ruff or two.

East returns the spade jack to my queen and West's ace. The moment of truth. Does East get a diamond ruff? No. Or at least, not just now. West returns the six of spades to the seven, eight, and my king. I start with trump by leading low towards the dummy. West is right there with the ace! Both East and I, who have already suffered through one moment of truth, get to suffer through another. Why did West have to have the ace of hearts? The wait takes only seconds but seems like forever. West doesn't get it right and returns a spade. I claim, sort of, since after drawing trump, I still have to take a diamond finesse, but that's the least of the worries on this hand.

COMPLETE HAND

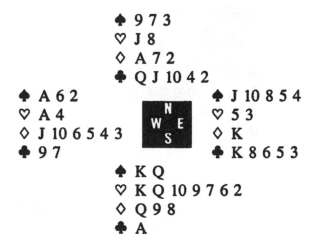

♠ 9 7 3
♡ J 8
◊ A 7 2
♣ Q J 10 4 2

♠ A 6 2
♡ A 4
◊ J 10 6 5 4 3
♣ 9 7

♠ J 10 8 5 4
♡ 5 3
◊ K
♣ K 8 6 5 3

♠ K Q
♡ K Q 10 9 7 6 2
◊ Q 9 8
♣ A

FURTHER ANALYSIS

Aside from a questionable two diamond bid, West's performance on this hand was much better than the result appeared. The hand could have been this instead.

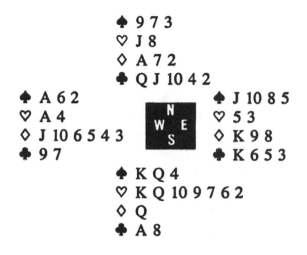

            ♠ 9 7 3
            ♡ J 8
            ◊ A 7 2
            ♣ Q J 10 4 2

♠ A 6 2   ♠ J 10 8 5
♡ A 4   ♡ 5 3
◊ J 10 6 5 4 3   ◊ K 9 8
♣ 9 7   ♣ K 6 5 3

            ♠ K Q 4
            ♡ K Q 10 9 7 6 2
            ◊ Q
            ♣ A 8

If this was the layout, declarer could be forgiven for taking the diamond finesse at trick one. A winning diamond finesse would save declarer from needing finesses in both clubs and spades. Note West's play of the ace of hearts. If South held the second hand, West had to grab the heart and cash a spade before it went on the ace of diamonds.

I think East contributed to West's error when he returned the jack of spades. It appeared East was trying to establish spade tricks when what he really wanted was a diamond ruff. A better play by East would have been the ten or eight of spades which would make spades less appealing to West.

East recovers some credit with an interesting observation to his partner. "Don't you think I would have raised diamonds with king third?"

Hand 22

BOTH VULNERABLE
SOUTH DEALS

South
♠ A Q J 8 2
♡ K 7
◇ Q 9 8
♣ A K Q

Hands like this are quite difficult to handle. One spade runs the risk of being passed out when game exists, and when partner responds one notrump, it's likely that the wrong hand will be declarer. I feel that most of these difficulties can be met if I open TWO NOTRUMP. I can lose the spade suit but I gain an accurate expression of value and I play it from the right side.

Alex does something unexpected. He transfers with THREE HEARTS showing spades. I'm expected to bid three spades but my hand looks good enough to take a slight overbid. FOUR SPADES. Alex bids FOUR NOTRUMP which is Key Card Blackwood: I answer with FIVE SPADES showing two aces and the trump queen. Alex raises to SIX SPADES, passed out. I'm not at all ashamed of my bidding but my hand is not especially good for slam purposes. All these points in spades are unnecessary. If Alex has the king fifth, my queen and jack won't have much practical value. The opening lead is the jack of hearts.

BOTH VULNERABLE
SOUTH DEALS

♠ K 9 7 6 5
♡ A 2
◇ A 7 2
♣ 10 8 4

```
  N
W   E
  S
```

♠ A Q J 8 2
♡ K 7
◇ Q 9 8
♣ A K Q

West	North	East	South
			2NT
Pass	3♡ (a)	Pass	4♠
Pass	4NT (b)	Pass	5♠ (c)
Pass	6♠	Pass	Pass
Pass			

(a) Transfer to spades
(b) Key Card Blackwood
(c) Shows two aces and the trump queen

LEAD: ♡J

This is a good slam. It would have been cold (almost) on a diamond lead and it is a tad better than a finesse otherwise. I win the king of hearts, East signaling with the eight. When I draw trump, West shows up with the singleton.

Eventually I have to make a play in diamonds, but in the meantime, I can afford to cash the three high clubs.

97

When I do this, West shows out quickly having started with J6 doubleton. This means West started with ten cards in hearts and diamonds.

This casts a pall on my original idea, which was to eliminate clubs and hearts, and then to play ace and a diamond. This would win whenever East has the king and when West has the king singleton or doubleton, and also when East has the jack-ten doubleton.

With West having ten red cards, the odds go up in favor of his having the diamond king. If he has four diamonds, he will have the king four times to East's three times. This comes to 57% of the time. If West has five diamonds, he will have the king five times to East's two times or approximately 71% of the time. This doesn't look good for my original plan.

OK, try plan two.

If I take the view that West has the king of diamonds, which looks to be about 60%+ I can try to endplay him by leading a low diamond from dummy to the nine. West will win and be obliged to lead a diamond. If he started with the king, success.

Having cashed the clubs, I play a heart to the ace and lead the diamond two, East plays the five and I play the eight. West wins the ten and leads a prompt diamond six. I don't see any reason to change my line so I finesse to my queen which wins. Plus 1430.

COMPLETE HAND

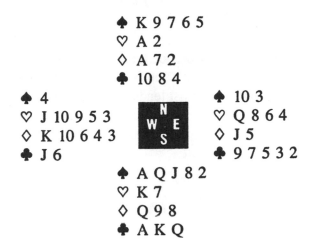

```
              ♠ K 9 7 6 5
              ♡ A 2
              ◇ A 7 2
              ♣ 10 8 4
♠ 4                         ♠ 10 3
♡ J 10 9 5 3                ♡ Q 8 6 4
◇ K 10 6 4 3                ◇ J 5
♣ J 6                       ♣ 9 7 5 3 2
              ♠ A Q J 8 2
              ♡ K 7
              ◇ Q 9 8
              ♣ A K Q
```

FURTHER ANALYSIS

In the end game, when I led the diamond, East had a chance to make a fine deceptive play. Had he inserted the jack, I would have to guess very well. If I judged the suit to be as it actually was I would have to play the queen and then finesse on the diamond return.

East's play of the jack opens up the possibility that he has the J10 or the J10x.

If East has J10, I can cover the queen losing to the king, but when West returns a diamond, I have to make an inspired guess.

If East has J10x, I have to duck and then play the nine when East returns his small diamond.

Clearly, if East plays the jack or ten of diamonds, I have to do some good guessing.

There is an interesting variation available to an astute East.

```
            A 7 2
10 6 5 3                    K J 4
            Q 9 8
```

It looks like I have one loser but looks can be deceiving. Say I lead the two and East plays the jack! If I decide he has J104, I must duck. Now when East leads the four, I would play the nine hoping for J10x, but losing to the actual layout.

Note East should be less quick to falsecard with Jxx than with 10xx. If this were the suit,

```
            A 7 2
K 9 6 3                    J 4 2
            Q 10 8
```

declarer might lead the two to the queen. If East plays the jack, what could be two defensive tricks would turn into one.

As I said in the introduction to this section, A72 opposite Q98 can be exciting!

Hand 23

NORTH/SOUTH VULNERABLE
EAST DEALS

South
♠ A 7 2
♡ A K J
◊ Q J 7 2
♣ J 9 7

East opens ONE SPADE. I'm going to bid something, but it's not clear to me which is best, one notrump or a double.

Both have flaws. One notrump suffers from a bad spade holding but exactly defines the strength and shape of the hand. Double may allow partner to declare notrump, but this is unlikely to happen. Also, if Alex bids a suit at the two level, I will feel like I have unshown values with no way to express them.

Even though double feels more awkward, I'm choosing it because of the specific danger of my spade holding for notrump. DOUBLE.

West PASSES and Alex responds with THREE DIAMONDS.

That friendly. East isn't through. He competes with THREE SPADES. I wish I could make a forcing pass, but it isn't available. I choose THREE NOTRUMP. My spade stopper hasn't gotten better, it's gotten worse. Alex has promised strength though and I can see a source of tricks in diamonds. Everyone PASSES and West leads the jack of spades.

NORTH/SOUTH VULNERABLE
EAST DEALS

```
              ♠ Q 9 8
              ♡ 8
              ◊ 10 9 8 6 5 4
              ♣ A K Q

                 N
              W     E
                 S

              ♠ A 7 2
              ♡ A K J
              ◊ Q J 3 2
              ♣ J 9 7
```

West	North	East	South
		1♠	Double
Pass	3◊	3♠	3NT
Pass	Pass	Pass	

LEAD: ♠J

Tricks all over. If I cover the spade I can get two spade tricks. I'm missing thirteen points and West has the jack of spades. The queen of hearts is surely onside since if not, it would leave East with an opening ten count. The heart finesse will give me three tricks. After I lose the ace and king of diamonds, I will have four tricks there and I have three club tricks immediately. A total of twelve tricks to choose from.

Will I have time to get them? Aside from diamonds, I have eight sure tricks so three notrump will require that I knock out the diamonds and at the same time keep RHO from using his spades.

What are my options? If I cover the jack of spades, and East covers too, can I succeed by ducking as I did on a previous hand? Assuming East does cover, and I do duck, East will lead another spade. I'll assume I can win the nine in dummy. When I lead diamonds, East will win and lead more spades. Unfortunately, on this hand, I know East has both diamond honors. He has enough entries that he can set up the spades and then run them.

It's possible that I can't make three notrump but there is still one avenue I haven't explored. It looks silly. It feels silly and it may be silly.

What if I duck the jack of spades in both hands?

If West has the stiff jack of spades, he won't be able to continue them and East will have to use both of his entries to set up the spades. He won't have an entry to cash them.

East ought to have six spades for his rebid. He has little enough.

I'm going to duck in both hands. East looks hopeful but West's thoughts are clearly on what to switch to. He leads the ten of hearts and I can pretty much claim losing to the ace and king of diamonds.

COMPLETE HAND

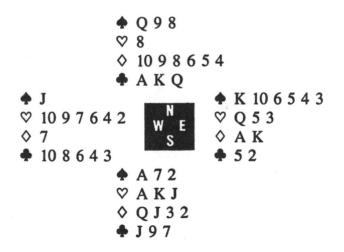

```
              ♠ Q 9 8
              ♡ 8
              ◊ 10 9 8 6 5 4
              ♣ A K Q
♠ J                           ♠ K 10 6 5 4 3
♡ 10 9 7 6 4 2      N         ♡ Q 5 3
◊ 7            W        E      ◊ A K
♣ 10 8 6 4 3       S          ♣ 5 2
              ♠ A 7 2
              ♡ A K J
              ◊ Q J 3 2
              ♣ J 9 7
```

FURTHER ANALYSIS

There is one more possibility that I did not look at.

```
            Q 9 8
  J 10                      K 6 5 4 3
            A 7 2
```

When West leads the jack, I can block the suit by covering. If East covers, I win. Now East gets in with a diamond and leads a spade to West's ten. West can't clear spades and East has only one entry left to set up the spades. He has no entry to use them.

If I cover and East ducks, I knock out a diamond. East will lead another spade but I'll duck it to West's ten. Again, the defense is an entry short to get the spades going.

Hand 24

South
- ♠ K 4 3
- ♡ A 7 2
- ◊ K Q 8
- ♣ A K 4 3

I open ONE CLUB. Alex responds ONE DIAMOND and I rebid TWO NOTRUMP. Alex raises to THREE NOTRUMP so we have achieved a simple sequence. West leads the jack of hearts.

NORTH/SOUTH VULNERABLE
SOUTH DEALS

- ♠ 7 5 2
- ♡ Q 9 8
- ◊ A J 10 4
- ♣ Q 8 2

```
    N
  W   E
    S
```

- ♠ K 4 3
- ♡ A 7 2
- ◊ K Q 8
- ♣ A K 4 3

West	North	East	South
			1♣
Pass	1◊	Pass	2NT
Pass	3NT	Pass	Pass
Pass			

LEAD: ♡J

105

I have eight sure winners and I can get a ninth in hearts. If clubs divide or if the ace of spades is onside I can end up with some overtricks.

The obvious danger is that East gets in and returns a spade. That could be bad for me.

I may end up playing a spade to the king, but I want it to be on my terms and not the opponents.

If West has made an honest lead, I can get my second heart trick without letting East in.

I cover the jack and East plays the king. I win and return a heart setting up my ninth trick. Only if West led from Jx will I fail and only then if they can run the spades.

West wins and continues hearts. East has played, in order, the king, three, and four. This implies he has the missing heart which is the five. If East did not have it, if he started with K43, he would have played the king, perforce, and followed with the four and three.

Now I have some options. If East has the ace of spades, I can get ten tricks by leading to my king of spades. I can also go down by doing this. I decide to take my nine tricks first starting with the clubs. If they are three-three I have ten tricks. If they are not three-three, I will run the diamonds and lead a spade. I will get ten tricks if East has the spade ace and not the thirteenth club and heart.

This line gets me only nine tricks, but under the circumstances, this is acceptable since carelessness or greed could have gotten less as I see.

COMPLETE HAND

♠ 7 5 2
♡ Q 9 8
◇ A J 10 4
♣ Q 8 2

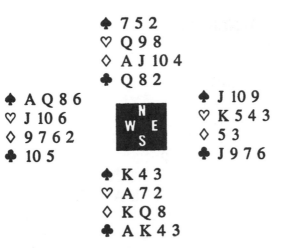

♠ A Q 8 6
♡ J 10 6
◇ 9 7 6 2
♣ 10 5

♠ J 10 9
♡ K 5 4 3
◇ 5 3
♣ J 9 7 6

♠ K 4 3
♡ A 7 2
◇ K Q 8
♣ A K 4 3

FURTHER ANALYSIS

Alex made a good bid of one diamond. Some would bid one notrump but that could suffer with a spade lead. If he had held,

♠ J 9 2
♡ Q 8 5
◇ Q 10 4 2
♣ A 8 7

one notrump would be correct.

In the play, the main problem was in playing the heart suit to keep East off lead. Compare this hand with the hand 19.

I commented that I knew East had the last heart from the way he played his spots. You may say this is a poor inference. The reason I trust this inference, and others like it, is that defenders have to communicate with each other. Good defense depends on an exchange of information. This requires a defender to be honest so as not to fool his partner. It's much more important for a defender to tell his partner what he does have than to fool declarer about something he doesn't have.

107

Hand 25

EAST/WEST VULNERABLE
WEST DEALS

South
♠ K 2
♡ Q 9 8
◊ 8 6 3
♣ 9 7 5 3 2

West opens ONE HEART which Alex DOUBLES. East PASSES so I must bid TWO CLUBS. Alex cue bids TWO HEARTS which can mean a number of things. Given I bid only two clubs the first time, I can bid TWO NOTRUMP now without overbidding my values. Alex raises to THREE NOTRUMP and everybody passes. West leads the queen of spades. I actually feel pretty good about this hand. I have goodish high card values and I have a fifth club.

EAST/WEST VULNERABLE
WEST DEALS

♠ A 8
♡ A 7 2
◇ A K Q J 5
♣ Q 6 4

♠ K 2
♡ Q 9 8
◇ 8 6 3
♣ 9 7 5 3 2

West	North	East	South
1♡	Double	Pass	2♣
Pass	2♡	Pass	2NT
Pass	3NT	Pass	Pass
Pass			

LEAD: ♠Q

Alex has a good hand. Barring something good happening though, it won't be good enough. Where is my ninth trick coming from?

One place is clubs. Perhaps I can set up the club queen.

Possible, but unlikely. West probably has both club honors, but since I can't lead twice toward dummy, I will need West to have the doubleton ace king. Also, with the defenders attacking spades, they may set up three tricks there. Only if West has QJ, QJ10, or QJ109 will the spade suit block.

I prefer to play for better chances if one can be found. The odds on both clubs and spades behaving are astronomically against me.

109

Can I do something with the heart suit?

If West had led them, I'd be cold for three notrump. I don't imagine I can convince West to lead hearts. Maybe I should lead them myself.

Can East have the king of hearts? I'm missing fifteen points so there is room for East to have three points. The king of hearts onside is barely possible.

Playing East for the king of hearts seems unlikely, although much better than the alternate line of West having the ace king doubleton club and the spades blocking.

Thinking about the hearts does open up another possibility which looks to be better, in fact, much better, than either line so far considered. Recently, I was reading about a play demonstrated by Mr. Chagas from Brazil. He called it an intrafinesse. I don't care what you call it, but if it will get another trick out of the air, I'll use it.

The 'intrafinesse' as it would apply to this hand, works this way.

```
          A 7 2
K 10 6 5 4          J 3
          Q 9 8
```

I start hearts by leading the two from dummy to my eight and West's ten. Later, I will lead the queen squashing East's jack.

This play will also work if the jack and ten of hearts are interchanged. It will not work if West has all three honors or if the suit divides four-three.

Also, if East plays the ten or jack on the first round, I must guess if he started with a singleton honor or jack ten doubleton. And, in what could be a memorably embarrassing moment, I might lose two tricks in this case.

```
          A 7 2
J 10 6 5 3          K 4
          Q 9 8
```

I lead the two, East plays the four!, and I finesse the eight losing to the ten. Now I lead the queen and . . . oh, well.

Back to the actual hand, I can't see anything better than the intrafinesse. It will work if East has the stiff ten or jack or the doubleton ten or jack. It will also work if East has the stiff king or if he has the doubleton king and plays it.

In order for the play to work, I must preserve my entry to lead the queen of hearts, so I must win the first trick in dummy. The heart two gets the five, eight, and jack. West continues the spade ten and I win. Now the heart queen. I hope Chagas knows what he's talking about.

Today he does. West covers, I play the ace, and East the ten. The darned thing worked.

COMPLETE HAND

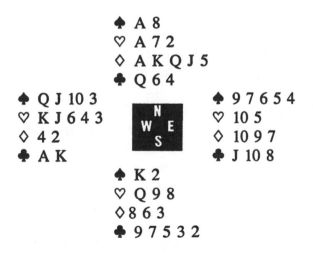

```
              ♠ A 8
              ♡ A 7 2
              ◇ A K Q J 5
              ♣ Q 6 4
♠ Q J 10 3              ♠ 9 7 6 5 4
♡ K J 6 4 3      N      ♡ 10 5
◇ 4 2         W   E     ◇ 10 9 7
♣ A K            S      ♣ J 10 8
              ♠ K 2
              ♡ Q 9 8
              ◇ 8 6 3
              ♣ 9 7 5 3 2
```

FURTHER ANALYSIS

It's amazing how often a second or third alternative turns out to be better than your initial thoughts.

Hand 26

NORTH/SOUTH VULNERABLE
WEST DEALS

South
♠ A K Q 9 7
♡ Q 9 8
♢ A K Q
♣ A K

West passes as does Alex and East. No one can quibble with
TWO CLUBS on this hand. West is not impressed. He bids
TWO HEARTS, no doubt with an eye on the vulnerability.
Alex PASSES and East does, too.

I wouldn't expect Alex to bid. There's nothing he can have.
But East's silence is a little surprising. East has a bad hand.
In circumstances like this one, East usually tries to preempt
the auction. Since he didn't, I expect him to have a balanced
yarborough with no fit for West's hearts.

I bid TWO SPADES. It wouldn't occur to me to bid any
number of notrump. Alex won't have many high cards, but he
could have spade support. It's even possible, although I doubt
it, that he has a singleton heart.

West PASSES and Alex raises to THREE SPADES. This
is good and unexpected news. The raise in our methods promises useful points. If Alex had a poor hand with support, he
would either jump to four spades, or if his hand was really bad,
he would make a second negative of three clubs and then raise
spades.

Since Alex has enough to raise, I know he does not have
a singleton heart. If he did, he would have made a splinter raise.
Actually, I make this about 95%. I suppose I could come up
with an example hand with a stiff heart which would not splinter,
say:

112

♠ J x x x
♡ x
◇ J x x x
♣ Q x x x

What should I bid now? It's possible four spades is our limit so I shouldn't go rushing to the five level. I cue bid FOUR CLUBS and Alex cue bids in return with FOUR HEARTS.

This convinces me I should bid to slam but it also opens the possibility of seven.

♠ J x x
♡ A x x
◇ x x x
♣ Q J x x

This hand makes seven notrump.

♠ 8 x x x
♡ A x
◇ x x x x x
♣ x x

This one might also make seven notrump although it would require diamonds to divide.

I have no idea how to get to seven. I can't tell partner that five diamonds to the jack are gold or that the jack of hearts is a big card. I decide to cue bid FIVE DIAMONDS. If Alex can cue bid the king of hearts, (hard to believe), or if he can cue bid a singleton ace of heart, (also unlikely) I will bid seven spades. Otherwise, I will guess to stop in six. Alex signs off in FIVE SPADES, so I follow my intentions and bid SIX SPADES. Possibly, I should bid six notrump. I wouldn't object to it at all.

West leads the jack of clubs. I do not get the dummy I was hoping for.

Alex though thinks he's got something and says he hopes we haven't missed seven. Don't worry, Alex. We are high enough.

NORTH/SOUTH VULNERABLE
WEST DEALS

♠ 6 5 4 3 2
♡ A 7 2
◇ 8 6 4
♣ Q 6

```
  N
W   E
  S
```

♠ A K Q 9 7
♡ Q 9 8
◇ A K Q
♣ A K

West	North	East	South
Pass	Pass	Pass	2♣
2♡	Pass	Pass	2♠
Pass	3♠	Pass	4♣
Pass	4♡	Pass	5◇
Pass	5♠	Pass	6♠
Pass	Pass	Pass	

LEAD: ♣J

Alex is entitled to his view. His queen of clubs could be a key card. As it is, it's worthless and my chances of even six spades are in jeopardy. Those five little spades are not helping either. If any one of them were a small club, I would make this. I win the club lead and draw two trump, West having one.

114

This hand is going to boil down to the heart suit. Possibly I should play it as I did in the previous hand with the help of the intrafinesse. Or perhaps I can endplay West as I did on hand 22.

Nope. Won't work. Even though dummy has five trump, I can't get there in order to play hearts from the dummy. I would like to start the heart suit by leading the two. Unfortunately, my only entry is the heart ace and that runs my intrafinesse position and my endplay position.

There are some other chances here and I'm going to look at them closely.

One possibility is to cash the clubs and diamonds and lead the nine of hearts. If West has the KJ10xx(x) he will cover and I will duck, endplaying him.

Since any line requires I cash the minors, I'll do it to see what happens.

West follows to all of my minor suit winners as does East. No strong distributional clues here.

Going back to my play of leading the nine of hearts and ducking when West covers, I see this play will also work if East has the stiff K, J, or 10. He will win and be endplayed. In essence, this play works whenever hearts are six-one.

If hearts are five-two, my line will work only if West has KJ10xx. It will fail whenever East has 10x or Jx, since he will win and return a heart.

The possibility that East has 10x or Jx opens up one more possibility, I can lead the queen. West must cover and I will win the ace. Another heart will endplay East if he started with 10x or Jx since he won't be able to unblock and West won't be able to overtake.

This queen play also wins when East has a singleton 10, J, or K. It only loses when West has KJ10 fifth or sixth.

I think I will try the queen. If the suit is five-two, the queen plays wins when East has an appropriate doubleton. Assuming West has the king, East's doubletons include:

J 10	10 6	6 5	5 4	4 3
J 6	10 5	6 4	5 3	
J 5	10 4	6 3		
J 4	10 3			
J 3				

If East has the J10, I make no matter what I do. Of the other fourteen cases, eight include Jx or 10x and the queen plays wins. Six cases include small doubletons and the queen play loses.

If hearts are six-one, I should lead the nine since I can never go down. Whoever wins is endplayed.

Are hearts six-one or five-two?

I would bet a fortune that hearts are five-two. If West had six, he might have opened with a weak two or even a three bid.

Not having done so, if he had six hearts, he would have preempted over my two clubs. It has become the style nowadays, and correctly so I think, to bid aggressively when your opponents open with a strong one club or strong two club bid. Why let the opponents have a free ride? It's unfair enough that they have all the high cards.

I'm playing for five-two and I lead the queen. West covers so I win it. East gives this a lot of thought. If he is thinking about showing out, I am down. No, he has hearts so I'm sure I've done the right thing. If East had a stiff heart, he would play it with no thought. The only way he could be thinking is if he started with 10x or Jx. East does play the ten after additional thought and I can claim, losing to the jack of hearts.

West observes that East has made a good thoughtful play and comments on it. Had my hearts been Q97 or worse, East's unblock would have been necessary.

116

COMPLETE HAND

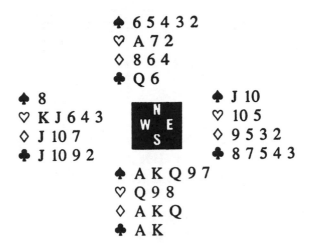

```
           ♠ 6 5 4 3 2
           ♡ A 7 2
           ◊ 8 6 4
           ♣ Q 6
♠ 8                          ♠ J 10
♡ K J 6 4 3       N          ♡ 10 5
◊ J 10 7        W   E        ◊ 9 5 3 2
♣ J 10 9 2        S          ♣ 8 7 5 4 3
           ♠ A K Q 9 7
           ♡ Q 9 8
           ◊ A K Q
           ♣ A K
```

FURTHER ANALYSIS

This hand is typical of those hands where you know you are cold if you could just guess the position.

Chapter 4

A 7 4 2			K J 5 3
	OR		
K J 5 3			A 7 4 2

Of the combinations in this book, this is the one mostly likely to be chosen as a trump suit. But it could just as well be a side suit at a trump contract or a crucial part of a notrump contract.

Usually you will cash the ace and then take a finesse. There will be reasons why you might choose to vary from this.

For instance

Hand 27

BOTH VULNERABLE
WEST DEALS

> *South*
> ♠ K J 5 3
> ♡ 10 2
> ◊ K 10 7 4 2
> ♣ A 8

West opens ONE HEART. Alex cue bids TWO HEARTS which is Michaels showing spades and an unknown minor suit. We play that you can do this on any strength hand on the theory that competitive auctions are easier if you get your shape across early.

East leaps to FOUR HEARTS. He may be hoping to lure me into taking a phantom save, but if so, he will be disappointed. I have a good hand and fully expect to make something. FOUR SPADES.

Whatever East had in mind must wait a moment because West rebids FIVE HEARTS. Alex PASSES, as does East, and I have to consider whether to bid again.

Hands like these are frustrating in that Michaels, which was supposed to help us, has actually gotten in our way. I don't know which side suit Alex has. If he has clubs, the opponents may be down a couple of tricks. If Alex has diamonds, they may make an overtrick.

I guess FIVE SPADES. This is passed out too fast to suit me. It smells like the opponents were both pushing and I have fallen for it.

West leads the queen of clubs. Alex's dummy gets mixed reviews.

BOTH VULNERABLE
WEST DEALS

♠ A 7 4 2
♡ 8 4
♢ A Q J 8 6 3
♣ 9

```
  N
W   E
  S
```

♠ K J 5 3
♡ 10 2
♢ K 10 7 4 2
♣ A 8

West	North	East	South
1♡	2♡ (a)	4♡	4♠
5♡	Pass	Pass	5♠
Pass	Pass	Pass	

(a) Michaels

LEAD: ♣Q

I had expected a fifth spade or at least better spades. I am not cold for this and worse, they can't make five hearts unless there are voids in both spades and diamonds. Someone may be void in diamonds, but there is no spade void because someone with Q10986 of spades would have chanced a double.

By the same token, I don't think anyone has four spades.

I take the club ace and play the spade ace and a second spade. West follows with the eight and East with the six and then the ten. Should I finesse?

I won't make five spades unless I pick up the trump suit. Either West has Qx or East has Qxx. I'm down if West has Qxx or if they divide four-one.

Assuming they are three-two, who has the queen? Is it possible to tell?

I check their lead card and it says they lead normally. East has the club king.

What else do I know? I don't think West has the ace king of hearts or he would have led one so East has a high heart honor and might have a lesser heart honor also.

This gives East six or more proven high card points. West ought to have the queen of spades to give him a twelve count opener.

Even though the odds favor a finesse, I'm playing for the drop.

When the queen comes down, I end up with an overtrick.

I note we would have gotten 800 if I had doubled. Plus 680 will be good, but plus 800 would have been better for both the score and the ego.

COMPLETE HAND

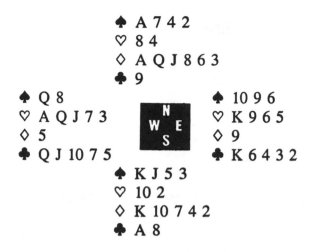

```
            ♠ A 7 4 2
            ♡ 8 4
            ◊ A Q J 8 6 3
            ♣ 9
♠ Q 8                          ♠ 10 9 6
♡ A Q J 7 3                    ♡ K 9 6 5
◊ 5                            ◊ 9
♣ Q J 10 7 5                   ♣ K 6 4 3 2
            ♠ K J 5 3
            ♡ 10 2
            ◊ K 10 7 4 2
            ♣ A 8
```

FURTHER ANALYSIS

The decision to drop the queen of spades in part depends on your opponents' bidding style. If West is known to open light hands, dropping the queen would be less clear.

In the bidding, Alex and I suffered a little from lack of definition. I had hoped for better or more spades. What Alex had wasn't wrong, but I was not aware he would do it with his actual hand.

Partnerships need far more understandings than just "15 to 17 partner, etc."

Hand 28

NO ONE VULNERABLE
SOUTH DEALS

South
- ♠ 3
- ♡ K J 5 3
- ◇ A K Q J 10 7
- ♣ 8 4

I open ONE DIAMOND. West overcalls ONE SPADE which Alex DOUBLES. This is a negative double promising four hearts. East raises to TWO SPADES. I have far too many tricks to bid three hearts only, so I take the plunge and bid FOUR HEARTS. West waits for three passes and leads the king of spades.

NO ONE VULNERABLE
SOUTH DEALS

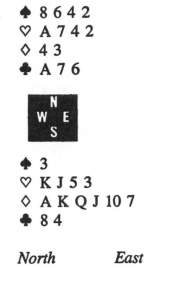

♠ 8 6 4 2
♡ A 7 4 2
◇ 4 3
♣ A 7 6

♠ 3
♡ K J 5 3
◇ A K Q J 10 7
♣ 8 4

West	North	East	South
			1 ◇
1 ♠	Double (a)	2 ♠	4 ♡
Pass	Pass	Pass	

(a) Negative Double

LEAD: ♠K

West leads the king of spades and continues a spade to East's ace. I ruff and start hearts by leading to the ace. This fetches the six and eight from West and East. East plays the ten on the next trump.

Finesse or not.

When opponents overcall as opposed to opening the bidding, their values are less clearly defined. On this hand, there is no reason to place the queen of hearts in either opponents hand.

Does this mean I should just finesse because it's the percentage thing to do?

No. Even at matchpoints, there are times when you should make sure of your contract. Hooking the heart is right if you

123

want to make six hearts. The king is right if you want to make five or four hearts.

See what happens if you finesse the jack and lose. West will lead another spade tapping you out of your king of hearts. You'll be able to cash some number of diamonds, but when the opponents come in with their high heart, your hand will be dead.

I play the king of hearts and when West follows small, I run the diamonds, conceding a later trick to the trump queen.

COMPLETE HAND

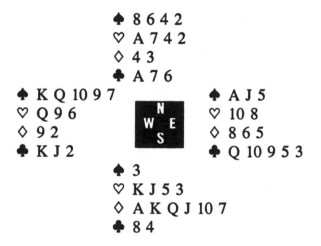

```
              ♠ 8 6 4 2
              ♡ A 7 4 2
              ◇ 4 3
              ♣ A 7 6
♠ K Q 10 9 7                    ♠ A J 5
♡ Q 9 6          N             ♡ 10 8
◇ 9 2          W   E          ◇ 8 6 5
♣ K J 2          S             ♣ Q 10 9 5 3
              ♠ 3
              ♡ K J 5 3
              ◇ A K Q J 10 7
              ♣ 8 4
```

FURTHER ANALYSIS

A small point in the auction. East raised to two spades. Not earth shattering, but important. Raising lets West determine whether to compete, save, pass, or double.

In the play, the jack of trumps is a trap. If declarer didn't have it, it would be routine to play two top hearts followed by diamonds.

Hand 29

EAST/WEST VULNERABLE
EAST DEALS

South
♠ A 7
♡ K J 5 3
◇ A K
♣ A K Q J 7

In second seat, I open TWO CLUBS and get the usual TWO DIAMONDS from Alex. I rebid THREE CLUBS rather than three notrump which would be my alternative. Alex bids THREE DIAMONDS which is a second negative. My choices now are three hearts, or three notrump.

I'm bidding THREE HEARTS which is sort of a guess. If Alex has four hearts, we should probably play in hearts.

If Alex doesn't have four hearts, he may be able to bid three notrump, possibly playing it from the wrong side, or he may be able to bid three spades allowing me to bid three notrump.

What I don't want to hear is a preference to four clubs.

Three notrump by me could be right, but it runs the risk that Alex has four hearts and nothing else.

Over my three hearts, Alex bids FOUR SPADES. Unexpected, but very welcome. This is a splinter bid showing a stiff spade and heart support. If Alex has the ace and queen of hearts, seven will be cold.

I can ask in two ways. I can start with 4NT Blackwood, or I can bid 5NT, the grand slam force.

Since Alex and I haven't discussed the grand slam force recently, I'm not sure what our responses would show. Fortunately, we have discussed Blackwood and its variations.

I ask with FOUR NOTRUMP and Alex shows an ace with FIVE DIAMONDS. Now I bid FIVE SPADES, asking him for the trump queen. If he has it, he bids six hearts, if not, five notrump.

Alex denies with FIVE NOTRUMP. If Alex had six hearts to the ace, seven hearts would be a good contract, but if he had that, he would have bid them over my three club bid.

I bid SIX HEARTS which closes the auction.

West leads the five of diamonds.

EAST/WEST VULNERABLE
EAST DEALS

♠ 2
♡ A 7 4 2
◇ 8 7 6 4 2
♣ 9 5 3

```
      N
   W     E
      S
```

♠ A 7
♡ K J 5 3
◇ A K
♣ A K Q J 7

West	North	East	South
		Pass	2♣
Pass	2◇ (a)	Pass	3♣
Pass	3◇ (b)	Pass	3♡
Pass	4♠ (c)	Pass	4NT
Pass	5◇	Pass	5♠ (d)
Pass	5NT (e)	Pass	6♡
Pass	Pass	Pass	

(a) Negative (d) Asking for the trump queen
(b) Second Negative (e) No trump queen
(c) Splinter

LEAD: ◇ 5

Alex's four spade bid has worked very well. East plays the queen of diamonds and I win the ace. I lead the heart three, the ten, the ace and East plays the six. The heart two gets East's eight. Should I finesse?

The danger in finessing is that West will win and give East a diamond ruff or even a club ruff.

Is either likely? The diamond ruff is unlikely because that would leave West with J10953 of diamonds. He would lead the jack from that holding.

As for East ruffing clubs, it's also unlikely. East might have doubled six hearts for a club lead.

Aside from losing an overtrick, are there any dangers in making the safety play of the king of hearts?

Yes. Extreme dangers. If I play the king and West shows out, I have to get back to dummy for another heart lead. I can only do this by ruffing a spade. When I lead dummy's last heart, East will win and tap me with a spade. I'll end up down about four tricks.

The king of hearts is as unsafety a play as I can imagine.

I finesse the jack and see it was necessary as West shows out. I claim losing a late trick to East.

COMPLETE HAND

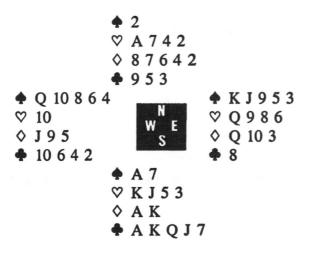

```
              ♠ 2
              ♡ A 7 4 2
              ◇ 8 7 6 4 2
              ♣ 9 5 3
♠ Q 10 8 6 4            ♠ K J 9 5 3
♡ 10          N         ♡ Q 9 8 6
◇ J 9 5     W   E       ◇ Q 10 3
♣ 10 6 4 2     S        ♣ 8
              ♠ A 7
              ♡ K J 5 3
              ◇ A K
              ♣ A K Q J 7
```

FURTHER ANALYSIS

If West had led a club, it is conceivable that it was an attempt to give East a ruff. Under these circumstances, South would have a slight reason to play the king of hearts.

In the bidding, Alex used three diamonds as a second negative. When opener rebids three clubs, it preempts the auction and makes it hard for North to show values. The three diamond bid is far more likely to conceal some hidden strength than, say this sequence.

North	South
—	2♣
2◊	2♡
3♣*	

*Bad hand

Three clubs is a true second negative. North has more room to show strength without getting beyond three notrump. For instance.

North
♠ 8 6 5
♡ J 6
◊ K J 8 7 5
♣ 5 4 2

North	South
—	2♣
2◊	2♡
3◊	

North can show a fair suit when opener rebids two hearts.

North	South
—	2 ♣
2 ◇	3 ♣
?	

North has no way to show diamonds and still try to keep three notrump open.

In the auction, I wanted to use the Grand Slam Force but didn't because I wasn't sure of our responses. This is just another example of the need to discuss conventions. The Grand Slam Force is rarely used but the prize for success is enormous and the price for confusion is disastrous.

Hand 30

NORTH/SOUTH VULNERABLE
WEST DEALS

South
♠ K Q 7 6 4 3 2
♡ 9
◊ K J 5 3
♣ 2

West opens ONE HEART which Alex DOUBLES. East bids FIVE HEARTS so I am faced with an unusual decision. My choices are easy. I bid five or six spades. Less easy is deciding which one.

I choose FIVE SPADES for two reasons. West did open the bidding and there is no reason to think he was kidding. I have a good hand but not that many high cards. West can have a full opening bid with two or even three aces. There is no reason why Alex should be the one with three aces.

Also, given the extreme bidding by East, This hand won't break well. Alex incidentally promises only three spades by his double.

Everyone PASSES ending the bidding as abruptly as it began. West leads the king of hearts.

NORTH/SOUTH VULNERABLE
WEST DEALS

                    ♠ A 8 5
                    ♡ 8 2
                    ◊ A 7 4 2
                    ♣ A J 7 3

                    ```
                     N
                    W   E
                     S
                    ```

                    ♠ K Q 7 6 4 3 2
                    ♡ 9
                    ◊ K J 5 3
                    ♣ 2

West	North	East	South
1♡	Double	5♡	5♠
Pass	Pass	Pass	

LEAD: ♡K

It turns out Alex is the one with three aces. That's good because it will make my task easier but I note that six spades is not a favorite and five spades is in minor jeopardy.

West follows the heart king with the ace and I trump it. East has played the ten and five.

When I ruff, West looks a little disappointed. I check his convention card. Four-card majors. This is a small and perhaps unimportant clue but I guess that East has six hearts.

The only danger to me is if West has four diamonds to the queen. I may be able to protect against that by beginning an elimination.

I cash the trump king and find them dividing two-one. I follow with the ace of clubs, a club ruff, a spade to the ace, and another club ruff. West turns up with the doubleton spade and has

131

followed with the K106 of clubs. I play to the ace of diamonds and lead another diamond. This is safe because if West has four diamonds, he will have no more clubs, East shows out so I just duck the diamond to West. He is left with red cards only so is endplayed.

Had East followed to the diamond, I would have had a guess. Probably I would have finessed. West could have had 2-5-2-4 shape leaving East with 1-5-3-4.

COMPLETE HAND

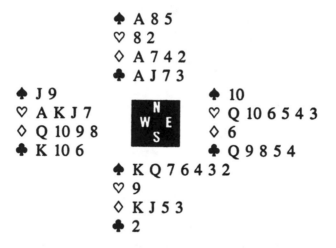

```
                    ♠ A 8 5
                    ♡ 8 2
                    ◊ A 7 4 2
                    ♣ A J 7 3
  ♠ J 9                            ♠ 10
  ♡ A K J 7          N             ♡ Q 10 6 5 4 3
  ◊ Q 10 9 8      W     E          ◊ 6
  ♣ K 10 6          S              ♣ Q 9 8 5 4
                    ♠ K Q 7 6 4 3 2
                    ♡ 9
                    ◊ K J 5 3
                    ♣ 2
```

FURTHER ANALYSIS

East made an excellent pressure bid when he bid five hearts. If he bid four hearts, it is a mortal cinch that someone would bid four spades. East's five heart bid essentially got him where he expected to go anyway. It made life difficult for us because we were forced to make a high level guess. Among other things the five heart bid meant I couldn't use Blackwood.

This hand offers an even better line for five spades if you wish to give up on the overtrick.

Ruff the second heart. Club ace and ruff a club. Spade king, spade to dummy's ace and ruff another club. (I'm assuming trumps are two-one.) Ace of diamonds and ruff the last club. This leaves

♠ 5
♡ —
◊ 7 4 2
♣ —

♠ Q
♡ —
◊ K J 5
♣

Trumps are gone and South is on lead. Lead the five of diamonds. If diamonds are three-two, you are home and if they are four-one, someone is endplayed.

This line would be best if you were playing IMPs or perhaps if you were doubled.

There are other variations. If West switches to a trump instead of another heart at trick two, you can't get your elimination.

133

Hand 31

> *South*
> ♠ J 10 7
> ♡ A Q J
> ◊ K J 7 3
> ♣ A K 3

In fourth chair I open a pushy TWO NOTRUMP. Alex raises to THREE NOTRUMP. West leads the spade two and Alex puts down a fairly crummy dummy. Given what I opened on, many dummys would look a little light so I can't complain.

**NO ONE VULNERABLE
WEST DEALS**

> ♠ 8 6 3
> ♡ 10 6 4 2
> ◊ A 5 4 2
> ♣ J 4

```
    N
  W   E
    S
```

> ♠ J 10 7
> ♡ A Q J
> ◊ K J 7 3
> ♣ A K 3

West	North	East	South
Pass	Pass	Pass	2NT
Pass	3NT	Pass	Pass
Pass			

LEAD: ♠2

East wins the ace and returns the nine. West cashes his four spades and on the last round I must find a discard from both hands. Before doing this, I have to decide where my nine tricks are coming from.

I have two major lines.

1. Play a diamond to dummy, finesse the jack, cash the king and reenter dummy with a diamond. Finesse in hearts and hope East started with doubleton king. Note that I must unblock in diamonds by leading the seven to dummy preserving the three for a fourth round entry.
2. Play the seven of diamonds to the ace and finesse in hearts. Play the king of diamonds dropping the queen (I hope) cash the jack and reenter dummy for another heart finesse.

Comparing these lines is fairly easy. A doubleton queen of diamonds in either hand is much more likely than a singleton or doubleton king of hearts in East's hand. Line two is two or three times better than line one.

In order for this line to work, I must keep four diamonds in both hands. On West's fourth spade I pitch dummy's two of hearts. Perhaps my apparent lack of interest will cause West to switch to hearts. East spoils this by signalling with the ten of clubs. I have no choice of discards from my hand. It must be the three of clubs.

West leads the seven of clubs which I win.

We'll see which way the wind is blowing. I lead the seven of diamonds to dummy and finesse the heart. So far so good. It wins. I cash the king and East drops the queen. More good news. When I get back to dummy with the fourth diamond, I repeat the heart finesse, which wins again. Nine nervous tricks.

COMPLETE HAND

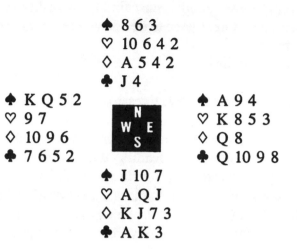

♠ 8 6 3
♥ 10 6 4 2
⋄ A 5 4 2
♣ J 4

♠ K Q 5 2
♥ 9 7
⋄ 10 9 6
♣ 7 6 5 2

♠ A 9 4
♥ K 8 5 3
⋄ Q 8
♣ Q 10 9 8

♠ J 10 7
♥ A Q J
⋄ K J 7 3
♣ A K 3

FURTHER ANALYSIS

Even though the diamond finesse worked, line one would have failed.

In the auction, I think Alex should have bid Stayman. It's not uncommon to open two notrump, with a five-card major. We could have had a five-four heart fit if not a four-four fit.

Hand 32

South
♠ K J 5 3
♡ 9 5 4
◊ —
♣ 10 8 6 5 3 2

When West opens THREE HEARTS Alex cue bids FOUR HEARTS and East raises to FIVE HEARTS.

I haven't heard this one lately.

We play four hearts as a Michaels cue bid and on this vulnerability Alex ought to have a fine hand. I bid FIVE SPADES and Alex finds extra values. He bids SIX SPADES. All pass and West leads the heart king.

♠ A 7 4 2
♡ —
♢ A K Q J 10 7 3
♣ K J

♠ K J 5 3
♡ 9 5 4
♢ —
♣ 10 8 6 5 3 2

West	North	East	South
3♡	4♡ (a)	5♡	5♠
Pass	6♠	Pass	Pass
Pass			

(a) Michaels

LEAD: ♡K

Alex has a nice hand. Good thing. I don't.

I haven't seen two voids in a while and I wish I weren't here. This hand would be easier to play if I had a diamond.

I have enough tricks if I can avoid a trump loser.

One heart ruff, four spades, and seven diamonds are enough. I don't have to ruff additional hearts.

The trouble is that I can't get my tricks if I make the normal play.

If I play ace of spades and hook the jack, I won't have an entry to run the diamonds.

Is there a way to overcome this? Yes. Save the entry until I need it. Assuming spades divide (I can't make against four-

138

one spades) and assuming the trump finesse wins, I can ruff the opening lead in dummy and take an immediate finesse in trump.

I do this and it wins. Losing would be bad but I can't help it. If West has the stiff queen, I was going down anyway and if he has Qx I would go down on the normal finesse.

When the jack wins I play the king of spades. I'm not out of the woods yet. West has to follow.

He does so I finish drawing trump and cash my twelve tricks.

COMPLETE HAND

♠ A 7 4 2
♡ —
◇ A K Q J 10 7 3
♣ K J

♠ 9 6
♡ A K J 10 8 3
◇ 8 6 2
♣ 7 4

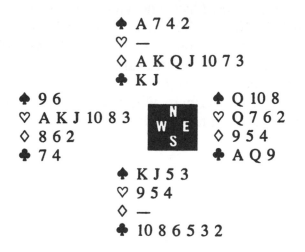

♠ Q 10 8
♡ Q 7 6 2
◇ 9 5 4
♣ A Q 9

♠ K J 5 3
♡ 9 5 4
◇ —
♣ 10 8 6 5 3 2

FURTHER ANALYSIS

This is a simple hand once you look ahead and see the traps of normal or instinctive play.

Hand 33

EAST/WEST VULNERABLE
EAST DEALS

South
♠ 10 4
♡ K 10 8 5 2
◊ K J 5 3
♣ A 7

East opens ONE CLUB. I have enough to act so choose the only realistic bid of ONE HEART. Alex cue bids TWO CLUBS which could mean nearly anything. I bid TWO DIAMONDS which doesn't promise or deny extra values. Notice how well defined our bids are.

Alex shows his intention with FOUR HEARTS. This is passed out. West starts with the club ten.

EAST/WEST VULNERABLE
EAST DEALS

                     ♠ K 6
                     ♡ A Q 9 3
                     ◊ A 7 4 2
                     ♣ J 3 2

                     ```
                        N
                     W     E
                        S
                     ```

                     ♠ 10 4
                     ♡ K 10 8 5 2
                     ◊ K J 5 3
                     ♣ A 7

West	North	East	South
		1♣	1♡
Pass	2♣	Pass	2◊
Pass	4♡	Pass	Pass
Pass			

LEAD: ♣10

Good spot. I'll make it if East has the queen of diamonds or if West has (unlikely) the ace of spades.

For the moment, I don't want West on lead to find a spade switch. To stop that, I cover the club and duck when East covers. I don't want West to have an entry with the nine of clubs.

My normal play would be to draw trump and play on diamonds hoping the queen is onside. I can add to this by arranging a position which can make even when the queen is offside.

I win the club continuation, and play the heart ace and king. These split with East having J7. Since I need to remove East's club exit, I play to the ace of diamonds and ruff the last club. East plays the king on this and West follows with the nine.

Should I go to dummy with a heart and finesse in diamonds?

No. This is an unusual position. If I do finesse in diamonds and they split I will end up losing two spade tricks.

I prefer to play the king of diamonds. If West or East drops the queen, I'm home. If no one drops it, I'll lead another diamond. Now, if West wins, the finesse was always offside and it didn't matter what I did. If East has the queen, I could have finessed, but the trick comes back because East is endplayed and I lose only one spade.

My play in effect breaks even if East has the queen and gains if West has Qx.

Before doing this, I have to confirm that East doesn't have four diamonds. If he does, then his fourth diamond would be an exit card on my line.

If East has four diamonds, I have to play ace, jack, king and throw East in with his last diamond. Again, he would be endplayed.

How many diamonds does East have? Is four possible?

Probably not. There are three decent reasons.

1. East might have opened one diamond.
2. West might have led a singleton diamond.
3. If East has four diamonds, West would have six spades. He might have bid over my one heart.

Satisfied that diamonds are three-two, I do play the king of diamonds with the best result possible. West has the doubleton queen.

I lose now my two spade losers so I end up making exactly.

COMPLETE HAND

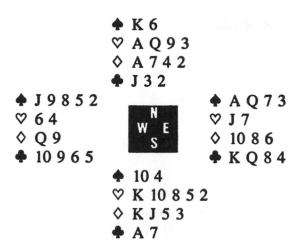

♠ K 6
♡ A Q 9 3
◇ A 7 4 2
♣ J 3 2

♠ J 9 8 5 2
♡ 6 4
◇ Q 9
♣ 10 9 6 5

♠ A Q 7 3
♡ J 7
◇ 10 8 6
♣ K Q 8 4

♠ 10 4
♡ K 10 8 5 2
◇ K J 5 3
♣ A 7

FURTHER ANALYSIS

Heads, I win. Tails, they lose.

Hand 34

BOTH VULNERABLE
EAST DEALS

South
♠ K J 5 3
♡ A 8 5 4
◊ 9 8 4
♣ K 10

East PASSES in first seat. I have a very close decision to open. I'm going to PASS mainly because my systemic choice would have to be one diamond. If I had three diamonds to the king and no king of clubs plus a ten spot more, I might open. Say the hand were:

♠ K J 9 3
♡ A 10 8 5
◊ K 10 8
♣ 5 4

I would be willing to open but would not insist. Any time you have a light hand, you must consider how the auction will go. If you can predict difficulties, you should pass. If you have easy rebids, go ahead and open. If you open the example hand above with one diamond, you will be ready for any response except two clubs.

The hand I am actually holding has too many flaws for a light opening so I do pass. West opens ONE CLUB and East responds ONE HEART. If my spades were better, I would overcall. Perhaps I should anyway.

I PASS and opener PASSES also.

Alex reopens with DOUBLE. I have a good hand but I respect that Alex is just reopening. ONE SPADE is enough. West

144

makes a delayed raise to TWO HEARTS passed back to me.
I compete with TWO SPADES and all pass.

West leads the ten of spades.

BOTH VULNERABLE
EAST DEALS

         ♠ A 7 4 2
         ♡ 10
         ◊ Q 6 5 2
         ♣ A 8 6 4

```
    N
  W   E
    S
```

         ♠ K J 5 3
         ♡ A 8 5 4
         ◊ 9 8 4
         ♣ K 10

West	North	East	South
		Pass	Pass
1♣	Pass	1♡	Pass
Pass	Double	Pass	1♠
2♡	Pass	Pass	2♠
Pass	Pass	Pass	

LEAD: ♠ 10

This is a good dummy. It has both four spades and a singleton heart. Since Alex could have doubled with three spades and two hearts or with fewer values, I am most appreciative of what he has. I also note that even with this dummy, four spades is extremely marginal. Two spades is high enough.

The easy and reflex play here is to let the spade ride around to my hand for a free finesse.

Since the obvious is so often wrong, I consider the consequences.

My play is certainly going to include ruffing hearts in dummy. If I duck the opening lead, it means one of my heart ruffs will be with dummy's ace of spades. That will promote a sure trick for East-West.

Strange as it feels, I think it better to win dummy's ace declining the finesse. Anyway, I can't imagine that West has led from the queen. If needed, I can take the finesse later so I won't lose anything.

I start with my plan playing the heart ace, a heart ruff. Club king and another heart ruff. Club ace, and a club ruff in my hand. When I lead my last heart, West follows and I get to ruff with dummy's last trump.

This leaves me with the KJ of spades and three diamonds. I lead dummy's last club and with East showing out I am able to get my jack of spades in. Ten tricks.

COMPLETE HAND

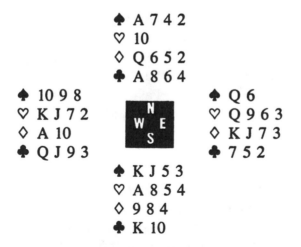

```
                 ♠ A 7 4 2
                 ♡ 10
                 ◊ Q 6 5 2
                 ♣ A 8 6 4
 ♠ 10 9 8                        ♠ Q 6
 ♡ K J 7 2          N            ♡ Q 9 6 3
 ◊ A 10          W     E         ◊ K J 7 3
 ♣ Q J 9 3          S            ♣ 7 5 2
                 ♠ K J 5 3
                 ♡ A 8 5 4
                 ◊ 9 8 4
                 ♣ K 10
```

FURTHER ANALYSIS

Note South's conservative approach in the auction. Few

146

things are more annoying and expensive than to balance and have partner hang you.

In the play, if declarer lets the spade come around to his jack, the defense can make him pay for it.

Declarer will play:

1. ♠J
2. ♡A
3. ♡ ruff
4. ♣K
5. ♡ ruff
6. ♣A
7. ♣ ruff
8. ♡ ruff with the ace
9. ♣8

This is the position at trick nine with dummy leading the eight of clubs: Declarer has won the first eight tricks.

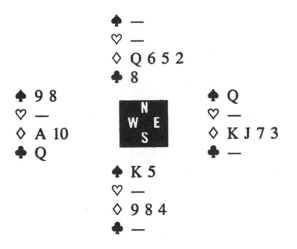

```
            ♠ —
            ♡ —
            ◊ Q 6 5 2
            ♣ 8
♠ 9 8              ♠ Q
♡ —       N        ♡ —
◊ A 10  W   E      ◊ K J 7 3
♣ Q       S        ♣ —
            ♠ K 5
            ♡ —
            ◊ 9 8 4
            ♣ —
```

On the club lead, East will ruff with the queen keeping declarer from scoring his little trump. South can delay by pitching a diamond, but with spades as they are, declarer gets nine tricks only.

Chapter 5

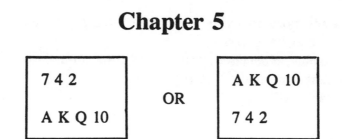

7 4 2	A K Q 10
A K Q 10	7 4 2

OR

This combination is almost always a notrump suit or a side suit. When it becomes trump it is mostly an accident and usually at the one or two level.

The most frequent question is whether to play the suit straight up, i.e., ace, king, queen, or whether it is right to play the ace, king and then finesse to the ten.

Hand 35

NORTH/SOUTH VULNERABLE
SOUTH DEALS

South
♠ A K J
♡ 9 4 3
◇ 10 5 4
♣ A K Q 10

This hand is not your basic one notrump opener because there are two completely unstopped suits. Even so, I choose ONE NOTRUMP because my alternatives leave me with impossible rebid problems.

Alex bids THREE NOTRUMP ending the auction. West leads the nine of spades.

NORTH/SOUTH VULNERABLE
SOUTH DEALS

♠ Q 10 2
♡ A K 6 5
♢ J 6 2
♣ 8 5 4

```
    N
  W   E
    S
```

♠ A K J
♡ 9 4 3
♢ 10 5 4
♣ A K Q 10

West	North	East	South
			1NT
Pass	3NT	Pass	Pass
Pass			

LEAD: ♠9

Having arrived in a good spot, I am pleased I opened one notrump. Had I opened one club, Alex would have bid one heart. I have no idea what I would have rebid.

Alex is still not using Stayman and I still don't agree with him. If you aren't going to bid Stayman, the reason should probably be that you have a terrible four-card suit. AK65 is very good.

The defense may have had five tricks in diamonds but with this lead I have nine tricks if I can bring in the club suit.

I win the king of spades and consider my options.

There are times when I might fool around with diamond plays but with such a good play for nine tricks, I'm going to try to take them.

149

The last thing I want to do is cash the high clubs now. I want to keep the opponents guessing as long as possible.

To do this, I cash the ace king of hearts first. Who knows? If a defender has a 4-1-4-4 hand, he might throw a club.

Next I cash the ace of spades. Again, I might get someone to pitch a club.

So far, everyone follows painlessly. I must play the top clubs now. I lead the king. Maybe someone will give me a count. I follow with the ace of clubs. Perhaps West will show out. No. West follows again. So far West has played 3, 7 and East the 6, 2. One of the defenders is lying.

I enter dummy with the queen of spades, all following, and lead the last club toward my Q10. East follows with the missing nine spot so I am cold for three notrump if I guess correctly.

Is it right to finesse on the theory that a four-two break is 48% and a three-three break is 35%?

Curiously, the correct play is the queen. By about two percent.

This suit combination is an example of how odds change in bridge as you get additional facts.

What facts do I have to influence my play? I know that of the four-two splits, there is no four-two split including a doubleton jack. Remember, I have cashed the ace and king and no one played the jack.

Here are the doubletons. There are fifteen of them.

J 9	9 7	7 6	6 3	3 2
J 7	9 6	7 3	6 2	
J 6	9 3	7 2		
J 3	9 2			
J 2				

We know that five of them do not exist. Only ten of the fifteen doubletons can exist.

If five of them can not exist, it obviously changes the chances for clubs to be four-two. The reduction is approximately one third. A four-two split is 48%. If you determine that five of the fifteen doubletons can not exist, the chances that one of the other four-two splits exist is about 32 percent.

This is all relative. At this moment you would say that the 35% chance for a three-three split is greater than the 32% chance of the POSSIBLE four-two splits.

I have no reason to go against the odds so I play the queen dropping the jack. The tiny percentage has worked.

Sometimes you have distributional information. If, in my three notrump contract, West had shown up with all seven spades and at least two hearts and two clubs, the odds would change to suggest the finesse was best.

COMPLETE HAND

```
              ♠ Q 10 2
              ♡ A K 6 5
              ◊ J 6 2
              ♣ 8 5 4
♠ 9 8 3                      ♠ 7 6 5 3
♡ Q 8 4        N             ♡ J 10 2
◊ A Q 9 3    W   E           ◊ K 8 7
♣ J 7 3        S             ♣ 9 6 2
              ♠ A K J
              ♡ 9 4 3
              ◊ 10 5 4
              ♣ A K Q 10
```

FURTHER ANALYSIS

I could just as well have cashed three spades first. This is more likely to get me a useful discard than on the sequence I tried. My plan was good but not as complete as it might have been.

Note that the combination AKQ10 opposite 854 is NOT the same as AKQ9 opposite 854.

A K Q 9

8 5 4

If you play the ace and king dropping the ten or jack from East, the odds are almost two to one that you should finesse. This is because all 10x combinations and all Jx combinations become crucial. With two pertinent combinations to consider rather than just one, the odds change drastically.

The *ACBL Bridge Encyclopedia* discusses this and similar combinations in six encyclopedia sized pages entitled "Restricted Choice."

I recommend these six pages to you.

Hand 36

South
♠ Q 7
♡ A 8 3
◊ K Q 8 5 4
♣ 8 5 4

East opens ONE SPADE. This isn't worth an overcall on any vulnerability so I PASS. So does West. Alex DOUBLES and I must find a descriptive bid. I'm torn between two and three diamonds. Since game requires Alex have a good hand I'm choosing the conservative TWO DIAMONDS. Alex raises me to THREE DIAMONDS so I can safely make a game try.

I just don't know what game try to make. If I bid three hearts, Alex can try for three notrump by bidding three spades. Or, he may bid three notrump himself.

Alternatively, I can bid three spades. Both of these approaches are uncertain because we won't be able to untangle half stoppers. For instance, if Alex has Jxx of spades, we have a stopper.

It is not within our partnership methods to do this perfectly so I guess to bid THREE HEARTS. I hope Alex doesn't raise to four hearts, but if he does, I'll pass.

Fortunately, Alex doesn't. He bids FOUR CLUBS. This is forward going but it implies two spade losers. I bid FOUR DIAMONDS. If Alex has enough for game he will bid it. I really had hoped to hear three notrump from Alex. For diamonds, my high cards are useful but my shape couldn't be worse.

Everyone passes and West leads the ten of spades.

♠ 8 2
♡ Q 5 4
◊ A J 6 3
♣ A K Q 10

```
  N
W   E
  S
```

♠ Q 7
♡ A 8 3
◊ K Q 8 5 4
♣ 8 5 4

West	North	East	South
		1♠	Pass
Pass	Double	Pass	2◊
Pass	3◊	Pass	3♡
Pass	4♣	Pass	4◊
Pass	Pass	Pass	

LEAD: ♠10

Twenty-seven high card points and we can't make a game and four diamonds isn't cold.

As it is, I consider stopping in four diamonds as good bidding. I wonder if we knew what we were doing.

East takes the king and ace of spades and exits with the ten of diamonds. Trumps are two-two.

If clubs run, I have ten tricks. I start them by playing the ace and king fetching small clubs from both defenders.

What now? Do I know enough that I should finesse the club or should I play the queen?

If I play the queen and East shows out, I am down since the auction tells me I have two heart losers.

How about if I hook the club? Do I go down if the finesse loses?

No, I don't. In this odd position, a losing club hook is not fatal because if it loses, East is endplayed.

I enter my hand with a trump and finesse the ten of clubs when West follows.

East does win but his heart return gives me one trick and the queen of clubs lets me get rid of my last heart.

COMPLETE HAND

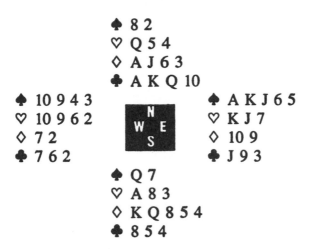

```
                ♠ 8 2
                ♡ Q 5 4
                ◊ A J 6 3
                ♣ A K Q 10
  ♠ 10 9 4 3                    ♠ A K J 6 5
  ♡ 10 9 6 2       N            ♡ K J 7
  ◊ 7 2          W   E          ◊ 10 9
  ♣ 7 6 2          S            ♣ J 9 3
                ♠ Q 7
                ♡ A 8 3
                ◊ K Q 8 5 4
                ♣ 8 5 4
```

FURTHER ANALYSIS

If West had shown out on the third round of clubs, I would have had two interesting answers.

1. Lead the ten of clubs and pitch a heart while East wins the jack. He will be endplayed.
2. Ruff dummy's last club and play heart ace and a heart to the queen. East has five spades at least, two diamonds, four clubs, and at most, two hearts.

155

If East wins the king of hearts (expected), he will have only spades left and must give me a sluff and a ruff.

The first line loses if East opened a ten count and has no king of hearts.

The second line loses if East has only four spades and somehow finds a third heart.

I make line one about 96% and line two 100%.

Hand 37

NORTH/SOUTH VULNERABLE
EAST DEALS

South
♠ 9 4 2
♡ K Q
◊ 8 5 4
♣ A K 7 6 3

East announces a skip bid and calls TWO HEARTS, weak. I take my ten seconds and PASS. West raises to THREE HEARTS. Alex DOUBLES and I must choose my bid.

Alex's double is takeout and given the auction, he may not have that good a hand. Alex should double if he has the right shape and any kind of decent hand.

My choices are pass, three notrump, four clubs, and five clubs. In a weak moment I might think of three spades, but I hope I would never do it.

I bid THREE NOTRUMP on the theory that it's game if I make it. Certainly, on my values it's possible.

The other game contract, five clubs will require a huge hand from Alex because my heart holding is so bad. If Alex has a stiff heart, my KQ will be completely redundant.

Three notrump ends the auction and West leads the three of hearts. Alex puts down his hand with confidence and I sense he expects me to make this.

NORTH/SOUTH VULNERABLE
EAST DEALS

♠ A Q 7 3
♡ 8 2
◊ A K Q 10
♣ 8 5 2

```
    N
 W     E
    S
```

♠ 9 4 2
♡ K Q
◊ 8 5 4
♣ A K 7 6 3

West	North	East	South
		2♡	Pass
3♡	Double	Pass	3NT
Pass	Pass	Pass	

LEAD: ♡3

East wins the heart ace and returns the jack to my king.

With the diamonds in view, there is nothing to gain by cashing black suit winners so I play the two high diamonds. East and West both play little diamonds. I wouldn't expect them to give me an honest count more than half the time. Not with the AKQ10 of diamonds in dummy where they can see them.

I come to my hand with the club ace to finesse the queen of spades. It wins. When I cash the ace of spades, East plays his second small one (5, then 6) and West drops the king (8, then K).

When I come to my king of clubs, East plays the jack and West the queen.

Now it's time to guess diamonds. I lead the eight and West follows with the seven. Finesse or drop?

Without clues, I should play for the drop. Do I have reason not to?

What I know for sure is that East has two spades, five or six hearts, two diamonds and two clubs.

I ask West what style weak twos they use and he tells me they tend to be traditional meaning good six-card suits.

If I can take East to have six hearts, he has one mystery card. It could be the spade jack or ten, the diamond jack, or the club ten. In practice, the one missing card will not be the spade jack. I know West has three spades, (East hasn't room for four spades) and he could not afford to throw the king unless he had the jack.

There are therefore three cards that East can realistically have. This makes the odds strongly in favor of the diamond finesse. I do finesse and it wins.

For whatever it's worth, I know the card that East has. Do you?

COMPLETE HAND

```
                    ♠ A Q 7 3
                    ♡ 8 2
                    ◇ A K Q 10
                    ♣ 8 5 2
  ♠ K J 10 8           N           ♠ 6 5
  ♡ 9 6 3         W        E       ♡ A J 10 7 5 4
  ◇ J 7 6 2           S           ◇ 9 3
  ♣ Q 9                             ♣ J 10 4
                    ♠ 9 4 2
                    ♡ K Q
                    ◇ 8 5 4
                    ♣ A K 7 6 3
```

FURTHER ANALYSIS

East's last card was surely the ten of clubs.

When I led to my king of clubs East dropped the jack and West the queen.

If West had the ten of clubs, it means that when I led the club to my hand, West was holding the Q10. Most defenders tend, in such circumstances to be ready to win the queen if declarer finesses the jack and they have their ten ready if declarer wins the king. When the play goes jack from partner and king from declarer, the defender can play either the queen or the ten because they are now equals. A few defenders will think to falsecard the queen, but those who do falsecard usually balk just a second while the realization sets in that the falsecard is okay.

Hand 38

NORTH/SOUTH VULNERABLE
EAST DEALS

South
♠ A 7 2
♡ J 10 9 8
◇ A 8 3
♣ 8 5 4

After two passes, West preempts with THREE DIAMONDS and Alex DOUBLES. East raises to FOUR DIAMONDS which poses a typical matchpoint problem. Because we play double would be responsive asking Alex to bid. I do not have the option of a penalty double. I'm not sure I would do that anyway.

My choices are to bid four hearts which is a slight overbid, to double which asks Alex to pick the major, or to pass hoping Alex will reopen with another double.

It's easy to reject the last possibility. If Alex does double, I won't be sure I should pass it and if I pull to four hearts, Alex won't know I have anything. Also, there is the slight risk Alex will pass four diamonds.

I'm going to bid FOUR HEARTS. If Alex is four-four in the majors, hearts will be fine. If Alex has four spades and three hearts so that we have two four-three major suit fits, I want to play in hearts. I would prefer that if we are forced to ruff diamonds, that we do not ruff them with the four card trump holding.

Alex bids FOUR NOTRUMP which is Key Card for hearts. I answer FIVE HEARTS which shows two aces (or one ace and the heart king) and denies the heart queen. I'm glad I can warn him about the queen of hearts. My hearts are biddable, but they are not great and Alex may be hoping for a better suit.

Alex mulls this over and announces a skip bid of his own. SEVEN HEARTS.

Everyone passes and while West chooses the opening lead I can reflect that Key Card Blackwood has a hidden benefit. I know Alex has the AKQ of hearts. He wouldn't bid seven without them. Therefore I don't have to worry that he has taken a chance with, say, AKxx.

I still have to worry that we can make thirteen tricks. When West leads the queen of diamonds I can see we are in contention to make this.

NORTH/SOUTH VULNERABLE
EAST DEALS

```
              ♠ K 10 4
              ♡ A K Q 6
              ◇ K 7
              ♣ A K Q 10

                   N
               W       E
                   S

              ♠ A 7 2
              ♡ J 10 9 8
              ◇ A 8 3
              ♣ 8 5 4
```

West	North	East	South
		Pass	Pass
3 ◇	Double	4 ◇	4 ♡
Pass	4NT	Pass	5 ♡ (a)
Pass	7 ♡	Pass	Pass
Pass			

(a) Two aces or one ace and the heart king

LEAD: ◇ Q

162

Alex has his bid. Possibly he should have chanced seven notrump. Glad he didn't.

Seven hearts has decent chances. I can make it (assuming hearts aren't five-zero) if the club jack drops and I make it if East has five spades and four clubs since he will be squeezed.

I win the king of diamonds and play the ace king of hearts which are divided three-two. I draw the last trump. East has the long trump and West, who had a doubleton trump, discards a diamond. Next the ace king of clubs. If the jack drops I have no further problems. No jack and no one shows out. My plan now is to cash the ace of diamonds, ruff a diamond, king of spades, and ace of spades to my hand. When I lead my last trump I hope East is squeezed in this hypothetical position.

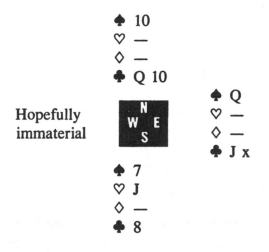

♠ 10
♡ —
◇ —
♣ Q 10

Hopefully immaterial

♠ Q
♡ —
◇ —
♣ J x

♠ 7
♡ J
◇ —
♣ 8

On the jack of hearts I will discard dummy's ten of spades and East will be finished.

If I pursue this line I will need to know if my seven of spades is high. The missing spades of consequences are the QJ98. I'll have to keep an eye out for them. It would be most embarrassing if I came down to this position and misread it.

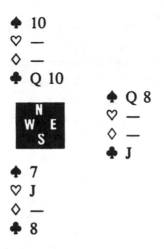

```
        ♠ 10
        ♡ —
        ◇ —
        ♣ Q 10
                      ♠ Q 8
           N          ♡ —
        W     E       ◇ —
           S          ♣ J
        ♠ 7
        ♡ J
        ◇ —
        ♣ 8
```

If I played the heart jack pitching the spade ten and East discarded the queen, I would need to know my seven was, in fact, not high.

Continuing with my line, I play the ace of diamonds, all following, and ruff my last diamond getting a small spade discard from East.

When I play the king of spades, West plays the nine and when I play the spade four to my ace, East plays the queen and West a diamond.

I cash my last heart discarding the spade ten and East, as envisioned, throws the jack of spades.

What now?

Because I reminded myself to pay attention to the QJ98 of spades, I know East still has the eight. I also know, perforce, that I am cold now because East can't have both remaining clubs. They are either three-three, or West possibly has both.

Do I know which?

Yes, and absolutely so. West has shown up with one spade, two hearts, six diamonds, and therefore four clubs. 100%. I finesse the ten and we score it up.

COMPLETE HAND

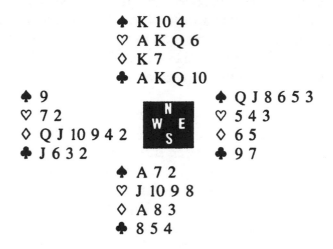

```
              ♠ K 10 4
              ♡ A K Q 6
              ◊ K 7
              ♣ A K Q 10
♠ 9                              ♠ Q J 8 6 5 3
♡ 7 2            N               ♡ 5 4 3
◊ Q J 10 9 4 2  W   E           ◊ 6 5
♣ J 6 3 2          S             ♣ 9 7
              ♠ A 7 2
              ♡ J 10 9 8
              ◊ A 8 3
              ♣ 8 5 4
```

FURTHER ANALYSIS

In the bidding, East's four diamond bid worked poorly for him. Had he passed, I would have been torn between three and four hearts. When he raised to four diamonds, I was able to bid four hearts without showing as much strength as if I had jumped to four hearts.

East's bid was not bad though. If I had held a different hand, say,

```
              ♠ K 6
              ♡ Q 10 8 7 5
              ◊ 5 4 2
              ♣ A J 3
```

I would have been delighted to jump to four hearts had I been able. Over 3 ◊, Double, 4 ◊, I would still bid four hearts but I would also feel I was doing an injustice to my hand.

From East's point of view, he expected me to have a better hand and he wanted to force me into making an underbid.

In the play, the potential for a squeeze was high and declarer had to foresee the position soon enough to start watching the spade spots. It turns out that the real trap in this hand was not to lose sight of one of declarer's most basic tools, i.e., the count. When spades were seen to be six-one, the last round of trumps was a waste of time. Enough was known that declarer could claim.

But not if he was lazy. If declarer didn't notice who had the last heart, the count would not have been known and the result would have, or could have been different.

Wakee, wakee.

One last observation. Since declarer could afford to draw all the trump without giving up various chances, it was wise to do so. If South had tried to ruff a diamond early, he would have gone down had East made an imaginative raise to four diamonds with just a singleton!

Hand 39

EAST/WEST VULNERABLE
WEST DEALS

South
♠ A K Q 10
♡ A
◊ A K 4 2
♣ A K 10 3

In fourth seat I am allowed to open the bidding. Courtesy probably of the vulnerability.

Strong 4-4-4-1 hands are best bid if you have a specific tool for them or if you have a strong one club system. The extra rounds of bidding are extremely valuable because you have so much to show.

Since we are using two clubs as our strong bid I must use it and do. TWO CLUBS. West clearly hitches before passing so I expect him to have something to think about.

Alex responds with TWO DIAMONDS.

My rebid is not clear to me at all. I remember a similar hand in the *Bridge World* some years ago. The Masters Solvers Club had lots to say but I don't remember the consensus.

I try TWO SPADES. Alex bids THREE CLUBS, our second negative and I show my diamond suit with THREE DIAMONDS. Alex shows he isn't entirely broke by jumping to FOUR SPADES.

That's good news of a sort but it doesn't make my decision any easier.

I expect Alex has three spades because he didn't bid four spades the round before, but that's not a sure conclusion.

If he does have three spades, it's possible that clubs, or even diamonds, is a better home. Unfortunately, either possibility is unattainable. Five clubs by me would be a cue bid and I don't expect Alex would have anything to show that would help me.

I bid SIX SPADES on the general value of the auction expecting it to have a play.

West leads the king of hearts showing that he had a little bit to think about earlier in the auction.

EAST/WEST VULNERABLE
WEST DEALS

♠ 8 5 4
♡ 2
◊ 7 6 3
♣ Q 9 8 6 4 2

	N	
W		E
	S	

♠ A K Q 10
♡ A
◊ A K 4 2
♣ A K 10 3

West	North	East	South
Pass	Pass	Pass	2♣
Pass	2◊ (a)	Pass	2♠
Pass	3♣ (b)	Pass	3◊
Pass	4♠	Pass	6♠
Pass	Pass	Pass	

(a) Waiting bid — may be negative
(b) True negative. No relations to clubs.

LEAD: ♡ K

This is an interesting dummy. Six clubs would have been better than six spades in the sense that it is cold. Six spades is a favorite, but it can go down.

At matchpoints, six spades is better than six clubs because

168

it will outscore six clubs whenever it is making. The best contract is six notrump since it too is cold. Seven of anything is more or less dependent on bringing home the spade suit. If the field were expert enough that everyone will reach a slam, it would be reasonable to bid seven clubs or seven notrump.

I settle down to deal with the contract that I am in, i.e., six spades.

Six spades is an unusual contract. Not many will find this four-three fit. Therefore, no matter how many tricks I take, I will be by myself. If I make exactly six, I lose to the six notrumpers, but I beat the six clubbers. If I make seven, then presumably, the six notrump declarers will also make seven so I will still lose to them.

This suggests that I do not worry about an overtrick because it will never matter except in comparison with a few other six spade bidders.

What dangers am I facing?

The obvious one is a five-one or six-zero trump split. I don't think I can handle either of these against good defense.

The next and more realistic danger is that spades are four-two. If I win the ace of hearts and lead out AKQ of spades, I'm in trouble if either defender started with Jxxx. I won't be able to run the club suit. The defense will wait and ruff in on the fourth round of clubs and will get two tricks at the end.

Is there any way to draw trump even against a four-two split?

There is no way to 'draw' trump but I can 'eliminate' them by conceding a trump trick early while there is still a trump in dummy to control the heart suit. One possible play is to enter dummy with the ten of clubs (unblocking) to the queen. I can finesse the spade and even if it loses, I can draw trump now and then run the clubs. There is a major danger to this line which I prefer to avoid. I don't need West to win the spade and then give East a club ruff.

I have an alternative play which loses one trick a large amount of the time but which improves my chances of taking twelve.

That play is to win the heart and at trick two to lead the ten of spades. Whichever defender wins, you can expect to win the return and draw trump and claim. This line loses if someone wins and gives the other defender a ruff. That would be unlucky, but you would pay off only when this occurred and only when you lose to Jx or Jxx of spades plus the ruff. If the defense started with Jxxx plus the mystery ruff, you weren't making anyway.

I do this, leading the ten of spades, and West takes it. He returns a spade and when East follows, I can draw trump and claim the rest.

COMPLETE HAND

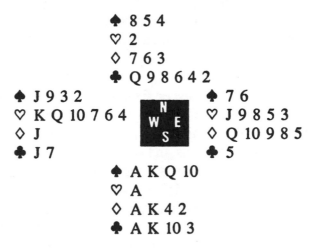

```
                ♠ 8 5 4
                ♡ 2
                ◊ 7 6 3
                ♣ Q 9 8 6 4 2
  ♠ J 9 3 2                    ♠ 7 6
  ♡ K Q 10 7 6 4               ♡ J 9 8 5 3
  ◊ J                          ◊ Q 10 9 8 5
  ♣ J 7                        ♣ 5
                ♠ A K Q 10
                ♡ A
                ◊ A K 4 2
                ♣ A K 10 3
```

FURTHER ANALYSIS

The safety play was necessary so if any other declarers end up in six spades, I have a chance to beat them if they were careless.

When I see West's hand, it occurs to me that I would have bid two hearts over two clubs even with the prevailing vulnerability. On this hand, East would have raised to three or four hearts. It turns out that five hearts, down 800, would be a good save against our slam.

Even though it did not occur, I am aware that my good hand would not have been easy to handle had West bid.

♠ A K Q 10
♡ A
♢ A K 4 2
♣ A K 10 3

West	North	East	South
Pass	Pass	Pass	2♣
2♡	Pass	Pass	?

OR

West	North	East	South
Pass	Pass	Pass	2♣
2♡	Pass	3♡	?

If either of these sequences occurred, I wouldn't be sure of what to do. Would double be for takeout or would it show a big notrump hand with a heart stopper?

What would it mean if, on the first sequence, I cue bid three hearts? Would that be a three suit takeout? Or could it possibly be natural intending to expose a psyche by West? Do you have clear agreements on these questions?

For that matter, do you know what your partner shows on any of these sequences?

West	North	East	South
			2♣
2♡	(2♠)		
	(2NT)		
	(3♣)		
	(Double)		
	(3♡)		

Does two spades show a suit of specific quality?

Does two notrump promise a stopper? Why didn't North double instead?

What kind of suit does three clubs show?

Does double show anything besides hearts? Could it be a negative double?

What does three hearts mean? Is it asking for a heart stopper?

If you find that your methods are undiscussed and therefore unsure, consider that your opponents may have similar difficulties. I have mentioned earlier in this book that bidding against strong bids is an effective strategy. You can use the above discussions to help you decide if this strategy will work for you.

Hand 40

BOTH VULNERABLE
EAST DEALS

South
♠ Q J 10 7 2
♡ 10 5 4
◊ A K Q 10
♣ 3

In second seat I open ONE SPADE. Alex responds THREE NOTRUMP which shows a balanced game forcing spade raise with four trump.

I have a close decision but choose FOUR SPADES. This gets passes out and West leads the ten of clubs.

BOTH VULNERABLE
EAST DEALS

♠ A 9 4 3
♡ A Q 6
◊ 8 5 4
♣ K J 2

```
    N
  W   E
    S
```

♠ Q J 10 7 2
♡ 10 5 4
◊ A K Q 10
♣ 3

West	North	East	South
		Pass	1♠
Pass	3NT (a)	Pass	4♠
Pass	Pass	Pass	

(a) Game forcing spade raise with four trump

LEAD: ♣10

Since there's no chance West is underleading the ace of clubs, I put in the jack losing to East's queen. East returns the two of diamonds and I win the ace, West playing the three.

My queen of spades loses to the king and the six of diamonds comes back. I win the king and West follows with the seven.

I draw trump with the ace and now have a choice of plays. I can insure the contract by ruffing dummy's little club, and playing the queen of diamonds. If the jack drops, I will pitch a heart on the ten of diamonds and take the heart finesse.

If the jack of diamonds does not drop I will ruff a diamond and lead the king of clubs. East will cover and I will pitch a heart leaving East on an endplay. This play guarantees the con-

174

tract but I'm going to do something else which I think increases my chance for an overtrick.

I expect the heart finesse to be onside because East has shown the spade king and the AQ of clubs. With the heart king, he would have opened the bidding.

Therefore, I can afford to take a diamond finesse expecting that if it loses, I will still make via the heart finesse.

Why not play the queen of diamonds which is the percentage play?

The reason I'm finessing is that East returned the two of diamonds. Most defenders play that the lead of a small card implies some strength and welcomes partner to continue the suit.

If East started with 962 of diamonds he could not afford the two because it might cause West to continue diamonds from Qxxx.

Defenders can not afford to send misleading messages to each other. Once in a while, declarer can take advantage, but that's the price of good defense. Win some, lose some, but come out ahead.

Also, if West had J73, he might (not a strong consideration), have encouraged. The diamond finesse works and as expected the heart finesse works, too. Plus 650.

COMPLETE HAND

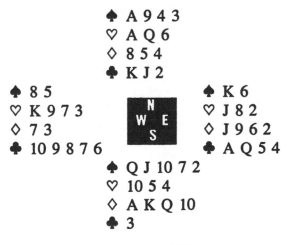

```
              ♠ A 9 4 3
              ♡ A Q 6
              ◇ 8 5 4
              ♣ K J 2
  ♠ 8 5                      ♠ K 6
  ♡ K 9 7 3                  ♡ J 8 2
  ◇ 7 3                      ◇ J 9 6 2
  ♣ 10 9 8 7 6               ♣ A Q 5 4
              ♠ Q J 10 7 2
              ♡ 10 5 4
              ◇ A K Q 10
              ♣ 3
```

175

I've repeated this theme before, but it's worth the emphasis. Defenders have to exchange information in order to be effective. If they don't, their defensive efforts will be more guesswork than informed decision making and the results will be ludicrous.

In the above hand, East led a low diamond. It is fairly standard that if a defender leads a low card he is expressing some interest in the suit.

This was the actual suit.

```
              8 5 4
    7 3                    J 9 6 2
              A K Q 10
```

East led the two and declarer eventually guessed to finesse the ten. This time the defense looked bad. But what if the suit had been like this?

```
              8 5 4
    Q 9 3                  ?
              ?
```

Say East leads the two and declarer wins the ace. When West gets in, should he return the suit.

If East has 762, West better not continue. But if East has J62 or K62, etc., it may be crucial for West to do so.

The point of this once again, is that defenders must use signals even at the cost of helping declarer on occasion. The long run benefits to the defenders make these signals necessary.

Chapter 6

K 10 2		6 4 3
	OR	
6 4 3		K 10 2

This is another of those combinations which may come under attack by your opponents or which you may have to play for yourself. In some settings, you may arrange for the opponents to lead the suit themselves, but at your convenience. Hopefully, this will never be your trump suit so there will be no such hands in this discussion.

Hand 41

NORTH/SOUTH VULNERABLE
SOUTH DEALS

South
♠ Q 10 9 6 5 3
♡ K 10 2
◊ A 8
♣ A 8

I open ONE SPADE and West overcalls TWO HEARTS. Alex cue bids THREE HEARTS which we play as a balanced game forcing spade raise. If Alex had a singleton somewhere, he would have used a splinter jump to show it. Since Alex has at least two hearts, I don't expect this hand to go anywhere so I bid FOUR SPADES which is intended to end the auction.

West has more to say with FIVE DIAMONDS. Alex bids FIVE SPADES and I PASS. I expect my hand is good enough to make five spades, but my heart values are worrisome and there could be a trump loser if East has the king.

West leads the queen of diamonds and I see my fears are groundless.

♠ A K J 4 2
♡ 6 4 3
◊ K 2
♣ K 7 5

♠ Q 10 9 6 5 3
♡ K 10 2
◊ A 8
♣ A 8

West	North	East	South
			1♠
2♡	3♡ (a)	Pass	4♠
5◊	5♠	Pass	Pass
Pass			

(a) Game forcing spade raise

LEAD: ◊Q

The trump suit is solid and the only possible losers are in hearts. I know if I play hearts myself I will lose three heart tricks, but I have a guaranteed line which will hold my heart losers to two.

I win the ace of diamonds and draw trumps which divide one-one.

Next I eliminate the clubs by playing ace, king, and ruffing the third round in my hand.

When I play to dummy's king of diamonds, this is the position.

♠ K J 4 2
♡ 6 4 3
◇ —
♣ —

♠ Q 10 9 6
♡ K 10 2
◇ —
♣ —

I lead the heart three and cover East's seven with the ten. West wins the jack but he can do no more than to cash the ace. Any play but a heart would give me a sluff and a ruff so West is over the proverbial barrel.

He chooses to cash the heart ace and I take my eleven tricks.

COMPLETE HAND

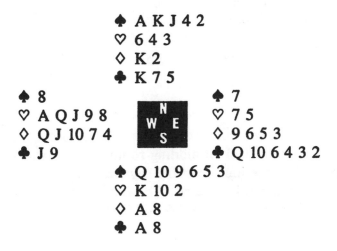

♠ A K J 4 2
♡ 6 4 3
◇ K 2
♣ K 7 5

♠ 8
♡ A Q J 9 8
◇ Q J 10 7 4
♣ J 9

♠ 7
♡ 7 5
◇ 9 6 5 3
♣ Q 10 6 4 3 2

♠ Q 10 9 6 5 3
♡ K 10 2
◇ A 8
♣ A 8

The end position is a common one as endplays go. Regardless of the location of the heart honors, the defenders can get only two tricks. If East plays the ace, the king is good. If East plays the queen or jack, you cover and even if West wins the ace, he must lead to your ten or he must give a sluff and ruff.

Note this position is not 100% if you are not able to eliminate the side suits. If the defenders have a safe exit, your endplay will be flawed.

Also, note that the ten of hearts makes the combination a 100% proposition. If you didn't have the ten, you would have a 50% chance instead.

$$\begin{array}{ccc} & 10\ 4\ 2 & \\ A\ Q\ 7\ 5 & & J\ 9\ 8 \\ & K\ 6\ 3 & \end{array}$$

Note also that if the ten is not in the hand with the king, the position is weakened a lot. In the above position, East will cover whatever card dummy leads and declarer will get no tricks.

In the auction, I commented that Alex's three heart cue bid promised a balanced hand. This was because he had room to make a jump cue bid if he wished.

If the sequence were:

West	North	East	South
			1♠
3♡	4♡		

North's four heart cue bid would show a game forcing spade raise, but because of lack of bidding room, i.e., no room for the jump cue bid, the four heart bid says nothing about shape or even about a control in hearts. These hands would all bid four hearts after the sequence 1♠ - 3♡ ?

♠ Q 10 8 7   ♠ Q 10 8 7   ♠ Q 10 8 7   ♠ K J 8
♡ 3   ♡ 3 2   ♡ A 8 7   ♡ 8 4 2
◇ K Q 8 7   ◇ K Q 8 7   ◇ J 3   ◇ A K 7 3
♣ A 6 4 3   ♣ A J 7   ♣ K Q J 6   ♣ K 10 7

Note the last hand has only three trumps. This is exceptional but acceptable because you have good high cards to compensate.

Hand 42

BOTH VULNERABLE
NORTH DEALS

South
♠ 6 4 3
♡ A K J 10 7 6
◊ A J
♣ A K

After two passes, I can choose from four possible openings. These are:

1. One heart
2. Two clubs
3. Two notrump
4. Four hearts

Of these, the only one worth rejecting is four hearts. The chances for slam are good and I'm not afraid of the opponents getting into the auction.

I'm going to choose TWO CLUBS but would not object much to two notrump. The reason I reject one heart is that there are too many little hands that will make a game. One heart could work though by keeping us out of an unmakable game but I regard it as pessimistic.

Alex responds TWO DIAMONDS and I rebid TWO HEARTS. Alex raises to THREE HEARTS. Should I make a slam try? Should I cue bid four clubs or diamonds or should I just bid game?

Since I don't want to get beyond game unless Alex has a super raise, I bid FOUR HEARTS which is, relatively speaking, a sign off. Alex has a minimum and passes so I play four hearts with the king of diamonds lead.

BOTH VULNERABLE
NORTH DEALS

```
          ♠ K 10 2
          ♡ Q 3
          ◇ 7 6 5 2
          ♣ 9 8 4 3
```

```
            N
         W     E
            S
```

```
          ♠ 6 4 3
          ♡ A K J 10 7 6
          ◇ A J
          ♣ A K
```

West	North	East	South
	Pass	Pass	2♣
Pass	2◇	Pass	2♡
Pass	3♡	Pass	4♡
Pass	Pass	Pass	

LEAD: ◇K

Alex's raise to three hearts was a thinking bid but it has gotten us to the wrong game. Three notrump is cold from either side and four hearts is not a lock.

I have nine easy tricks and the tenth must come from spades. There's no way I can come down to a position like I did in the previous hand. I'm going to have to play spades myself.

At trick one I win the ace of diamonds and draw trump in three rounds.

Now to get after a spade trick. Should I just lead to the king and hope?

I could, but there's a much superior play available, courtesy of the ten of spades. If I lead a spade toward dummy's K102,

183

I can play the ten rather than the king. If West has the queen and jack, East will be forced to win the ace.

If East wins with the jack or queen, I can still lead toward the king. This gives me a combined chance of around 62 percent which is a worthwhile improvement over the even money chance that West has the ace.

In fact, when I lead the three of spades, West plays the jack. I cover with the king and East wins the ace.

This is promising since West would not play the jack without the queen too.

When I later lead toward the ten of spades, West takes his queen so the ten becomes my tenth trick.

COMPLETE HAND

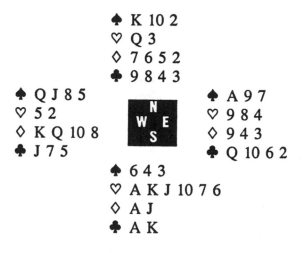

```
                ♠ K 10 2
                ♡ Q 3
                ♢ 7 6 5 2
                ♣ 9 8 4 3
  ♠ Q J 8 5                    ♠ A 9 7
  ♡ 5 2          N             ♡ 9 8 4
  ♢ K Q 10 8   W   E           ♢ 9 4 3
  ♣ J 7 5         S            ♣ Q 10 6 2
                ♠ 6 4 3
                ♡ A K J 10 7 6
                ♢ A J
                ♣ A K
```

FURTHER ANALYSIS

This delaying play in spades where you first try for the unlikely before committing yourself to your main chance is a standard bridge technique where you combine your chances.

Hand 43

NO ONE VULNERABLE
SOUTH DEALS

South
♠ 5
♡ J 10 9 7 6 5 2
◇ A Q
♣ 6 4 3

I open THREE HEARTS on the theory that I will have two confused opponents and only one confused partner. This hand is not classic but I feel better about bidding now than I would if I passed and came in later.

Alex likes hearts and his raise to FOUR HEARTS is passed out.

West leads the eight of diamonds.

NO ONE VULNERABLE
SOUTH DEALS

```
♠ A 8 4 2
♡ A K Q
◇ 9 6 3
♣ K 10 2
```

```
      N
   W     E
      S
```

```
♠ 5
♡ J 10 9 7 6 5 2
◇ A Q
♣ 6 4 3
```

West	North	East	South
			3 ♡
Pass	4 ♡	Pass	Pass
Pass			

LEAD: ◇ 8

This lead gives me ten sure tricks but it can never hurt to take eleven.

If I wish to take a casual view, I can draw trump and play on clubs leading to the ten and then later to the king. I may be able to do better by trying for an elimination. If I could get rid of all the spades and diamonds and then lead clubs, I could end up with an endplay as on the first hand in this section.

Do I have enough entries to do this and still have a trump in both hands?

I can't quite do that because I'm short of entries. But I can come close if I start right away.

The play goes:

1. ◊ 8 to the king and my ace.
2. ♠ 5 to the ace.
3. Ruff a spade.
4. Heart to the ace (both follow).
5. Ruff a spade.
6. ◊ Q.
7. Heart to the king.
8. Ruff a diamond.

So far, both opponents have followed suit throughout except for West pitching a spade on the second heart.

In this position I lead the three of clubs.

```
        ♠ 8
        ♡ Q
        ◊ —
        ♣ K 10 2



        ♠ —
        ♡ J 10
        ◊ —
        ♣ 6 4 3
```

West plays low and the ten loses to the queen. If East has the remaining spade he will have a safe exit. Otherwise he will be endplayed.

East cashes the club ace which confirms the endplay has worked.

COMPLETE HAND

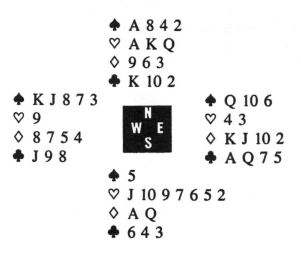

♠ A 8 4 2
♡ A K Q
◇ 9 6 3
♣ K 10 2

♠ K J 8 7 3
♡ 9
◇ 8 7 5 4
♣ J 9 8

♠ Q 10 6
♡ 4 3
◇ K J 10 2
♣ A Q 7 5

♠ 5
♡ J 10 9 7 6 5 2
◇ A Q
♣ 6 4 3

FURTHER ANALYSIS

South, by eliminating the spades and diamonds as he did achieved what is known as a partial elimination. If East had a fourth spade, the elimination would not have worked but South would not have lost anything because he could still lead clubs himself.

The important thing was to realize the potential for the elimination and to start it before drawing even one round of trump. The trump entries were a necessary part of the elimination. They were too valuable to use as entries to squander them solely for drawing trump.

As for my preempt of three hearts, it was not a bad bid on this vulnerability. The suit was good, if not full of high cards, and the outside strength was good offensively. Compare these two hands.

♠ 5   ♠ Q 5
♡ J 10 9 7 6 5 2   ♡ Q 9 7 5 4 3 2
◇ A Q   ◇ J 5
♣ 6 4 3   ♣ Q 7

Both hands have seven points and seven hearts but that's the last of the comparisions. The first hand has tricks. The second hand has losers. In the second hand, any one of the side honors may take a defensive trick, but they won't take an offensive trick unless partner puts down some combining high cards.

Hand 44

BOTH VULNERABLE
EAST DEALS

South
♠ K Q J 9 7
♡ 6 4 3
♢ A
♣ K Q J 10

In second seat I open ONE SPADE and Alex raises to TWO SPADES. I'd like to make a game try but no useful try exists. Three clubs would encourage Alex if he had the ace of clubs but if he has three or four small ones, he won't like them. Since I have the KQJ10, it really doesn't matter what Alex has in clubs. Other game tries include three hearts but that would cause Alex to like his Qxx of hearts when, in fact, it would be of little value. I'm going to go ahead and bid FOUR SPADES. It may not make but since the defense won't know what I have, they may not defend accurately.

West starts with the queen of diamonds which is good news. I would hate to have seen the queen of hearts.

BOTH VULNERABLE
EAST DEALS

        ♠ A 5 2
        ♡ K 10 2
        ◊ 5 4 3
        ♣ 8 6 4 2

         N
       W E
         S

        ♠ K Q J 9 7
        ♡ 6 4 3
        ◊ A
        ♣ K Q J 10

West	North	East	South
		Pass	1♠
Pass	2♠	Pass	4♠
Pass	Pass	Pass	

LEAD: ◊ Q

It looks like I have better than average chances of making this. If I can hold my losers to one club and two hearts, I'm home. In isolation, the heart suit offers me a sixty-two percent chance of getting a trick so my chances in total look good.

Unfortunately, there is a flaw in this hand. If the spades don't divide three-two, I may get tapped out before I can establish the club suit and my heart trick.

When I lead trumps, they divide three-two which is a significant hurdle. I draw three rounds of trump since I don't want anyone to get a club ruff and start on the club suit.

When I lead the king of clubs, East takes the ace and returns the king of diamonds. I ruff with my next to last trump. It's time to come to some conclusion about the heart suit. Should I lead to the ten or the king?

The answer is strictly one of economy. If I lead to the ten of hearts and it loses to the jack or queen, the defense will tap my last trump. The defender with the ace of hearts will be able to cash a diamond when he gets in so my tenth trick will be unattainable.

Since I can't afford to make the ideal play in hearts (low to the ten and then low to the king), I am obliged to do what I can which is to lead a heart to the king.

It wins and four spades makes but the difficulties of the hand make me wonder if my bid was correct.

COMPLETE HAND

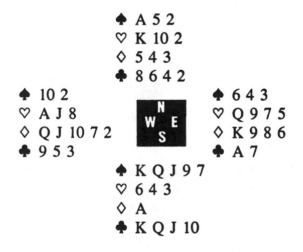

```
                 ♠ A 5 2
                 ♡ K 10 2
                 ◊ 5 4 3
                 ♣ 8 6 4 2
  ♠ 10 2                        ♠ 6 4 3
  ♡ A J 8            N          ♡ Q 9 7 5
  ◊ Q J 10 7 2    W   E        ◊ K 9 8 6
  ♣ 9 5 3            S          ♣ A 7
                 ♠ K Q J 9 7
                 ♡ 6 4 3
                 ◊ A
                 ♣ K Q J 10
```

FURTHER ANALYSIS

This hand represents the interesting fact that few things in bridge are as they seem. Every item must be judged as much on the surroundings as on the item itself. In theory, declarer's play in hearts was wrong, but since other options were precluded, it was the best play available.

In the bidding, my four spade bid was abrupt but not outrageous. The final contract wasn't as good as you'd like it to be. But since the auction was uninformative, I might get some vigorish back from the opening lead.

If West leads a trump, I gain a tempo. If West leads a club, I gain a tempo if the defense doesn't get a ruff. Also, West might lead a heart giving declarer an extra tempo. The heart queen from QJ98 would not be a defensive success.

You can get all kinds of opinions telling you that you need such and such odds before bidding a game. What they don't tell you is that the defenders often do something to change these odds. The less you tell the opponents, the more likely they will do something 'wrong.'

Hand 45

EAST/WEST VULNERABLE
NORTH DEALS

South
- ♠ A J
- ♡ Q J 6 2
- ◊ A K J 10
- ♣ 6 4 3

After two passes, I open ONE NOTRUMP. Alex's raise to THREE NOTRUMP ends the auction and West leads a menacing queen of clubs.

**EAST/WEST VULNERABLE
NORTH DEALS**

♠ K Q 5
♡ 10 9 5
◊ Q 9 6 4
♣ K 10 2

```
  N
W   E
  S
```

♠ A J
♡ Q J 6 2
◊ A K J 10
♣ 6 4 3

West	North	East	South
	Pass	Pass	1NT
Pass	3NT	Pass	Pass
Pass			

LEAD ♣Q

For a change, Alex doesn't have a four-card major. Too bad. If he had a fourth spade, I would have nine tricks.

As it is, I have seven sure tricks, one which I can develop in clubs for eight, and two in hearts if I can get them. The danger is that the opponents will get three clubs and two hearts first.

Is there anything I can do to slow the defenders down?

Yes. In some circumstances, I can break the opponents communications by ducking the opening club lead.

For instance

```
              K 10 2
Q J 9 8                      A 7 5
              6 4 3
```

If I cover, East wins and returns the seven. West will duck and the defense gets three clubs and two hearts.

If I duck, West will continue and I will finesse the ten losing to the ace. East can clear the suit, but if West has no heart entry, he can't cash his long club.

The chance that West has no heart honor is 25%, so it is worthwhile hoping for such a chance.

```
              K 10 2
Q J 9 8 7                    A 5
              6 4 3
```

If this is the layout and I duck, East will win the second trick as before but he won't be able to clear the suit. West won't be able to use the clubs unless he has both heart honors.

```
                    K 10 2
A Q J 9 8                        7 5
                    6 4 3
```

If West has led from this holding, ducking the lead works whenever West has no side entry, in this case, the ace or king of hearts.

The only danger to ducking is if West has led from Qx and I consider this to be impossible given our auction.

I try the duck and the queen wins. West continues with the nine which I finesse to East's ace. East switches to the heart three which implies the clubs are five-two. When the heart honors turn out to be divided, I can scramble home with nine tricks.

COMPLETE HAND

```
              ♠ K Q 5
              ♡ 10 9 5
              ◊ Q 9 6 4
              ♣ K 10 2
♠ 10 7 2          N          ♠ 9 8 6 4 3
♡ A 4         W     E        ♡ K 8 7 3
◊ 8 3 2           S          ◊ 7 5
♣ Q J 9 8 5                  ♣ A 7
              ♠ A J
              ♡ Q J 6 2
              ◊ A K J 10
              ♣ 6 4 3
```

FURTHER ANALYSIS

This blocking play can be used in a suit contract also although your goal will be to stop a ruff instead of stopping them from setting up a suit.

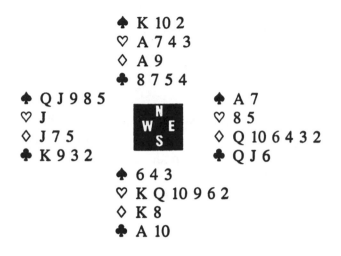

♠ K 10 2
♥ A 7 4 3
♦ A 9
♣ 8 7 5 4

♠ Q J 9 8 5
♥ J
♦ J 7 5
♣ K 9 3 2

♠ A 7
♥ 8 5
♦ Q 10 6 4 3 2
♣ Q J 6

♠ 6 4 3
♥ K Q 10 9 6 2
♦ K 8
♣ A 10

Against four hearts, West leads the queen of spades. Declarer has to decide if West has QJ in which case he must cover, or if West has QJ985 in which case he must duck to stop a third round ruff. QJx or QJxx won't make a difference.

In practice, declarer should probably duck, unless he has information to the contrary. Who knows, he may gain a bonus trick when West has QJxxxx opposite stiff ace.

Hand 46

NO ONE VULNERABLE
EAST DEALS

> *South*
> ♠ A K Q 10 9
> ♡ 6 4 3
> ◇ A K J 9
> ♣ J

East PASSES and I open ONE SPADE which West DOUBLES. Alex raises me to TWO SPADES which does not show much of a hand in our methods. Nonetheless, I will consider it unlucky if we can't make game so I go to FOUR SPADES. This gets passed out without a protest and West leads the king of clubs.

NO ONE VULNERABLE
EAST DEALS

♠ J 8 7 2
♡ K 10 2
◊ Q 4
♣ 9 8 7 5

```
    N
 W     E
    S
```

♠ A K Q 10 9
♡ 6 4 3
◊ A K J 9
♣ J

West	North	East	South
		Pass	1♠
Double	2♠	Pass	4♠
Pass	Pass	Pass	

LEAD: ♣K

On the king of clubs, East encourages with the six and West continues with the ace which I ruff.

I can afford one round of trump and when both opponents follow, I can afford another. Spades divide two-two. If I wish, I can run my diamonds discarding hearts, concede a heart, and claim, making five.

Or, I can be greedy. If I wish to take the risk that East has the ace of hearts, I can try to sneak a heart by West. If I can do this I'll be able to pitch dummy's two remaining hearts on the diamonds and make six.

It looks safe to try this because West rates to have the heart ace almost all the time. If he doesn't have it, he would either not have doubled, or East would have bid.

Since matchpoint rewards for overtricks are substantial, I do try a heart even though I may go down to game when I was actually cold for an overtrick.

West is having none of it. He takes his ace and I claim.

COMPLETE HAND

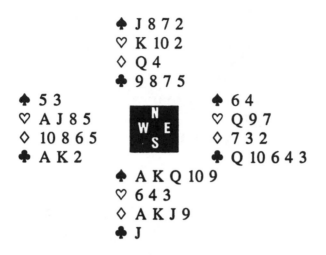

```
              ♠ J 8 7 2
              ♡ K 10 2
              ◊ Q 4
              ♣ 9 8 7 5
♠ 5 3                          ♠ 6 4
♡ A J 8 5          N           ♡ Q 9 7
◊ 10 8 6 5     W       E       ◊ 7 3 2
♣ A K 2            S           ♣ Q 10 6 4 3
              ♠ A K Q 10 9
              ♡ 6 4 3
              ◊ A K J 9
              ♣ J
```

FURTHER ANALYSIS

When I ask West why he was in such a rush, he pointed out that if I had the queen of hearts, I could finesse dummy's ten. He had no reason to wait.

Note that if trumps were three-one, my correct play would be to cash three diamonds, throwing one heart from dummy, and then lead toward the king of hearts. It would do me no good to discard two hearts on the diamonds because I would still have two heart losers and only one trump in dummy.

I commented that East couldn't have the ace of hearts. That would leave the East-West hands looking something like:

♠ 5 3   ♠ 6 4
♡ Q J 8 5   ♡ A 9 7
◊ 10 8 6 5   ◊ 7 3 2
♣ A K 2   ♣ Q 10 6 4 3

Most West players would not double and many East players would bid three clubs.

Chapter 7

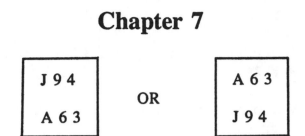

This is one of those combinations which you will postpone having to play as long as possible. It will be much easier for you if the opponents lead this suit or if you can pursuade them to lead it later.

Hand 47

BOTH VULNERABLE
WEST DEALS

South
♠ 10 5 2
♡ A 6 3
♢ Q J 10 9 4
♣ A K

West opens ONE CLUB and East responds ONE HEART. This hand is good enough to overcall on but its bad shape limits its potential. I'm bidding TWO DIAMONDS but it's not just because I have a decent hand. I'm bidding because my over-call will make it hard for West to make his normal rebid. My overcall will be especially annoying to him if he wanted to rebid one spade. If I catch opener with something like

♠ A K J 2
♡ Q 4 3
♢ 2
♣ Q J 10 8 6

he will have to pass or raise to two hearts. In both cases, he won't be able to show the main emphasis of his hand.

When West PASSES, Alex raises to THREE DIAMONDS. It might be right to pass or it might be right to bid. I don't have strong feelings. What I do feel is that if we have a game, it will be three notrump and not five diamonds.

Since three notrump isn't outlandish and since I have no good way to get Alex's opinion, I just bid it. THREE NOTRUMP ends the auction and West leads the jack of clubs.

BOTH VULNERABLE
WEST DEALS

```
              ♠ Q J 4 3
              ♡ J 9 4
              ◊ A 8 6 5
              ♣ 8 2

                 N
              W     E
                 S

              ♠ 10 5 2
              ♡ A 6 3
              ◊ Q J 10 9 4
              ♣ A K
```

West	North	East	South
1♣	Pass	1♡	2◊
Pass	3◊	Pass	3NT
Pass	Pass	Pass	

LEAD: ♣J

Not the dummy I was hoping for. I don't mind that three notrump is a poor contract. What's bad is that three diamonds will probably make.

East signals at trick one with the seven and I win the king. I may as well find out if the diamond finesse is working so I lead the queen and it wins. West covers the jack so I am up to eight tricks. The diamonds break two-two which may or may not matter. I doubt it is important.

Is there any chance of a ninth trick? Sometimes it is best to accept a small minus and not compound it with silly heroics.

Spades is an obvious source of more tricks, but there isn't time to get them. If I lead spades, the defense will get two spades and at least three clubs.

The heart suit has some slim potential though. My chances for a second heart trick are small, but if a miracle exists, I will get a second trick soon enough to enjoy it.

There are various ways I can get a second heart trick.

```
                J 9 4
   Q 10 8 7 5 2              K
                A 6 3
```

This can't exist because East bid hearts.

```
                J 9 4
   10 8 7 5 2               K Q
                A 6 3
```

This can't exist either for the same reason. but the next combinations are possible.

```
                J 9 4
   K Q                      10 8 7 5 2
                A 6 3
```

This is possible. All I need to do is play the ace and another heart, or better yet, duck a heart and then play the ace.

```
            J 9 4
Q 10                        K 8 7 5 2
            A 6 3


            J 9 4
K 10                        Q 8 7 5 2
            A 6 3
```

And so can these two combinations exist. but the winning
line is more complicated.

South must lead low toward the dummy. If West plays his
Q (or K) declarer later goes to the dummy and leads the jack
blotting out West's ten.

If West plays the ten dummy covers, East wins, and West's
honor now falls on declarer's ace.

Since West can have KQ, Q10, or K10, I come to my hand
with a diamond and lead the heart three. If West plays a prompt
queen, I will credit him for KQ (hopefully). If West stutters
before taking his king or queen, I will tend to play him for K10
or Q10. And, of course, if West plays the ten I'll have no choice
but to play him for honor ten doubleton.

I do all this and when I lead the heart three, West gives it
a little flicker and plays the queen. Since the flicker suggests
a choice of plays, I'm going to play him for Q10.

West continues clubs to my ace. I cash another diamond and
play to dummy's eight spot.

I still have time to change my mind and play West for KQ
of hearts.

I'm going with my original intentions. West is twice as likely to have Q10 or K10 than KQ. The principle of restricted
choice tells me that even after seeing one of West's cards he
is still more likely to have started with one of two special combinations rather than another single specific combination.

Following this principle, I lead dummy's jack. East ducks
and I must face the reality that if I finesse and lose, I may not

get another trick. That's life. Anyway, if I have done the wrong thing in hearts I'm going down one no matter what I do. Down one won't be worth much since we can make three diamonds and they can't make anything.

I let the heart go and West offers an annoyed ten spot. Restricted choice has worked.

COMPLETE HAND

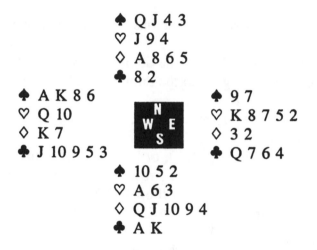

```
              ♠ Q J 4 3
              ♡ J 9 4
              ◊ A 8 6 5
              ♣ 8 2
♠ A K 8 6                      ♠ 9 7
♡ Q 10          N             ♡ K 8 7 5 2
◊ K 7        W     E          ◊ 3 2
♣ J 10 9 5 3    S             ♣ Q 7 6 4
              ♠ 10 5 2
              ♡ A 6 3
              ◊ Q J 10 9 4
              ♣ A K
```

FURTHER ANALYSIS

West had a minimum so he wasn't too unhappy at losing his one spade rebid. But if East had held,

```
♠ Q J 4 3
♡ K 8 7 5 2
◊ 3 2
♣ 7 5
```

they would have sold out to two or three diamonds when three spades was perhaps cold.

206

Hand 48

BOTH VULNERABLE
SOUTH DEALS

> *South*
> ♠ A 6 3
> ♡ Q J 9 7 3
> ◊ K 9 2
> ♣ A 4

I open ONE HEART and Alex bids ONE NOTRUMP. Since this is forcing in our system, I must rebid something. TWO DIAMONDS is mandatory so I bid it and I buy it.

West leads the three of diamonds.

BOTH VULNERABLE
SOUTH DEALS

> ♠ J 9 4
> ♡ 5 2
> ◊ A 7 6 5 4
> ♣ J 10 7

```
    N
  W   E
    S
```

> ♠ A 6 3
> ♡ Q J 9 7 3
> ◊ K 9 2
> ♣ A 4

West	North	East	South
			1 ♡
Pass	1NT (a)	Pass	2 ◊
Pass	Pass	Pass	

(a) Forcing

LEAD: ◊ 3

If diamonds are three-two, I have six possible losers and that's assuming I don't lose two clubs. To avoid this I will have to ruff a club in my hand.

At trick one I win East's ten with the king and play ace and a club. West wins the king and leads the eight of diamonds. I take the ace, East playing the jack. When I ruff dummy's club, West discards the six of hearts.

It looks like down one, but strange things have happened before. Perhaps something will happen here. I exit with the queen of hearts to West's king. West cashes the queen of diamonds, showing he led from Q83 and leads the king of spades.

It's apparent that West has been endplayed somehow and I have to wonder if West just led an honest card or is he falsecarding me.

I have seen West holds three diamonds and two clubs. If he had five spades, he would have overcalled. Therefore he has at least four and possibly five hearts.

If he did not have the ace of hearts also, he would, or should, have ducked my queen.

Therefore I am inclined to place West with the spade king, heart ace and king, diamond queen, and the club king.

I win the king of spades and return a spade. The defenders may be able to avoid leading further spades so I have to return one now and try to guess if West has led from KQx or K10x if, indeed, he has led from either.

West plays low leaving me to guess. I guess the nine playing West for K10x. There are two good reasons for this.

1. If West had the queen, he would have 17 points according to my hypothesis and he might have overcalled one notrump.
2. With KQx of spades, he might have led the king instead of the three of diamonds.

When I play dummy's spade nine, East wins the queen so some of my thoughts seem to have added up correctly.

COMPLETE HAND

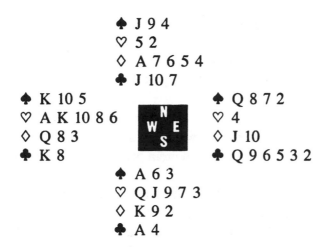

♠ J 9 4
♥ 5 2
♦ A 7 6 5 4
♣ J 10 7

♠ K 10 5
♥ A K 10 8 6
♦ Q 8 3
♣ K 8

♠ Q 8 7 2
♥ 4
♦ J 10
♣ Q 9 6 5 3 2

♠ A 6 3
♥ Q J 9 7 3
♦ K 9 2
♣ A 4

FURTHER ANALYSIS

Whatever West's reasons for a trump lead, it was deservedly effective. With good hearts, West could envision my ruffing hearts in dummy. I like his lead.

In the bidding, West erred I think by not overcalling with one notrump. Trap passing doesn't work as often as its advocates claim. Much better to bid when you can rather than to wait for the rare penalty. Note that on this hand, East-West can make three clubs and with a few small changes could make three spades. The trap pass here only cost a partscore swing. It might have cost a game.

Hand 49

NO ONE VULNERABLE
EAST DEALS

South
♠ 6 5 4
♡ A 6 3
◊ A Q J 10 9 8 3
♣ —

East opens TWO CLUBS which is a surprise and a disappointment. I imagine he and I have a grand slam. Too bad we can't get together.

I'm not quite sure what to bid here. If they were vulnerable, I'd bid five diamonds, but given no one is vulnerable, I think that's too much. My aces suggest their maximum will be a game only so I don't want to go for an excessive number.

I compromise with FOUR DIAMONDS. West PASSES and Alex offers FIVE DIAMONDS. East takes his time to make a mixed emotion DOUBLE. This is passed out and West leads the three of spades.

NO ONE VULNERABLE
EAST DEALS

♠ Q 9 2
♡ J 9 4
◊ K 6 5 4
♣ 9 6 4

♠ 6 5 4
♡ A 6 3
◊ A Q J 10 9 8 3
♣ —

West	North	East	South
		2♣	4◊
Pass	5◊	Double	Pass
Pass	Pass		

LEAD: ♠3

Who knows. They may be cold for six clubs. Or they may not have a game.

Alex was right to bid five diamonds since he could not know I nearly had a two bid of my own. The result is that I am going for three hundred at least and must avoid going for five hundred.

East takes the jack, king, and ace of spades with West playing the ten on the third round.

East switches to the king of clubs. I'm going to ruff this and try somehow to find a way to hold my heart losers to one.

There are various ways I can do this. I can play East for the stiff queen or king or the doubleton king queen. Also, if I eliminate clubs, I can play East for KQx of hearts and get him in an endplay. If I can get to this hypothetical ending I can avoid a second heart loser.

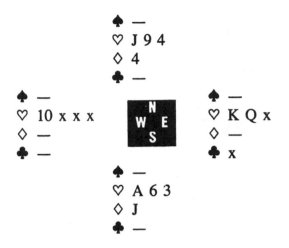

When I lead the heart three to the nine, East will win but have no good play.

I don't have to commit myself right away. I can try for the endplay and later still decide which heart combination I want to try for.

In order to get my endplay, I have to ruff three clubs. One I can ruff now but in order to ruff two more, I need two entries to dummy. These can only come from trump. In order for this to happen, I must save my three of diamonds for later use. Therefore I ruff the club high, i.e., anything except the three.

I choose the eight. I could as well ruff with the ace but I don't want to tell the opponents my suit is solid. Not that it will be a secret for long.

When I lead the nine of diamonds to the king, they divide one-one. I ruff another club high and enter dummy with the three to the four. I ruff dummy's last club and now have to decide the heart distribution in this position.

♠ —
♡ J 9 4
◇ 6 5
♣ —

♠ —
♡ A 6 3
◇ A Q
♣ —

With South on lead I must choose from low to the nine, hoping for an endplay, or leading the ace hoping East has

1. Stiff Q.
2. Stiff K.
3. ANY doubleton heart honor which will leave East endplayed.

I know East has three spades and may have four. He has one diamond exactly. If East has one or two hearts then he has six or seven clubs.

I'm inclined to think East is more likely to have three hearts just on general principles.

If he does have three, I have to take the first option of leading low to the nine. I do this and East wins the king. I finesse his heart return and it wins. Down three hundred.

COMPLETE HAND

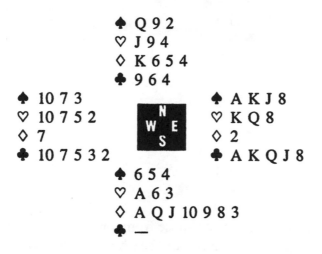

```
                    ♠ Q 9 2
                    ♡ J 9 4
                    ◊ K 6 5 4
                    ♣ 9 6 4
♠ 10 7 3                            ♠ A K J 8
♡ 10 7 5 2          N              ♡ K Q 8
◊ 7              W     E            ◊ 2
♣ 10 7 5 3 2        S              ♣ A K Q J 8
                    ♠ 6 5 4
                    ♡ A 6 3
                    ◊ A Q J 10 9 8 3
                    ♣ —
```

FURTHER ANALYSIS

Even if I had misguessed the heart distribution, my play would have worked if East had KQ doubleton or a singleton honor.

East could have gotten one more trick by switching to his diamond at trick four.

Hand 50

NORTH/SOUTH VULNERABLE
EAST DEALS

South
- ♠ A Q
- ♡ Q J 6 4 2
- ◊ 9 6 2
- ♣ J 9 4

East opens TWO SPADES, weak, which I PASS. I'm not close to having a bid but I won't mind if Alex can bid something. West raises to THREE SPADES which Alex DOUBLES.

Under the circumstances I have a good hand. It would be even better if my spade strength were in the minor suits, but my heart holding is superb. I bid FOUR HEARTS and I expect it to be cold or, at worst, down one. The only reason for concern is that Alex may have made an aggressive bid. The opponents have threatened to steal the pot and it's imperative for the person in Alex's seat to get into the auction. Often the only way in is to make a light double based on shape and a prayer.

NORTH/SOUTH VULNERABLE
EAST DEALS

♠ 4 2
♡ A 8 7 5
♢ A K 7 3
♣ A 6 3

```
  N
W   E
  S
```

♠ A Q
♡ Q J 6 4 2
♢ 9 6 2
♣ J 9 4

West	North	East	South
		2♠	Pass
3♠	Double	Pass	4♡
Pass	Pass	Pass	

LEAD: ♠ J

Alex has a good hand but four hearts is not cold.

I win the opening lead with the queen and lead the queen of hearts. West covers so I win and draw a second round. West started with the K109 so I have a trump loser.

It occurs to me that the AQ of spades are not doing me that much good. If they were instead the heart ten and the queen jack of diamonds, four hearts would now be cold.

I am faced with four possible losers. If diamonds divide three-three, I can pitch a club. I can add a little bit to this chance by trying for a partial elimination.

I cash the spade ace and the diamond ace. East drops the ten on this. Now, instead of playing king and another diamond,

I lead the three. If diamonds are three-three, I've lost nothing, but if East has Q10, QJ, or J10, he may be endplayed.

When I lead the three of diamonds, East takes the queen and leads the two of clubs. My nine forces West's queen so I am now cold, regardless of who has the king of clubs.

I cash the king of diamonds, succeeding whenever they are three-three. When East discards a spade, I ruff the last diamond and lead a heart to West.

West has no successful option. The defense gets their club trick, but that's it.

COMPLETE HAND

```
              ♠ 4 2
              ♡ A 8 7 5
              ◇ A K 7 3
              ♣ A 6 3
♠ J 10 5                    ♠ K 9 8 7 6 3
♡ K 10 9         N          ♡ 3
◇ J 8 5 4      W   E        ◇ Q 10
♣ Q 8 5          S          ♣ K 10 7 2
              ♠ A Q
              ♡ Q J 6 4 2
              ◇ 9 6 2
              ♣ J 9 4
```

FURTHER ANALYSIS

Alex had full values for his double. As I noted during the auction, this is one of the sequences where it is necessary to be extremely aggressive.

When the auction starts with 2♡, Pass, 3♡? or 2♠, Pass, 3♠? the fourth player should act almost as if he is balancing as opposed to bidding directly.

Everyone knows that the three heart bid is going to be passed by opener so, in effect, a bid by anyone should be balancing in nature. For example, the auction goes 2♡, Pass, 3♡?

♠ Q 10 7 3
♡ 3
♢ K J 8 7
♣ A J 5 4

Double. In sequences like this one, the hand with good shape has to take the aggressive action. On the auction 2♡, Pass, 3♡? it is clear to double. By comparision, if your RHO opened 2♡, it would be unclear to double.

Hand 51

EAST/WEST VULNERABLE
NORTH DEALS

South
♠ J 3 2
♡ K 4
◊ 8 6 5 3 2
♣ A 6 3

Alex opens ONE HEART and I respond with a forcing ONE NOTRUMP. Alex rebids TWO CLUBS which could be a three-card suit. I have a comfortable preference to TWO HEARTS and when Alex bids TWO NOTRUMP I have no qualms about bidding THREE NOTRUMP.

West, in spite of Alex's club bid leads the five of clubs.

EAST/WEST VULNERABLE
NORTH DEALS

♠ A 4
♡ Q J 10 9 7
◊ A K 4
♣ J 9 4

```
    N
  W   E
    S
```

♠ J 3 2
♡ K 4
◊ 8 6 5 3 2
♣ A 6 3

West	North	East	South
	1 ♡	Pass	1NT (a)
Pass	2 ♣ (b)	Pass	2 ♡
Pass	2NT	Pass	3NT
Pass	Pass	Pass	

(a) Forcing
(b) Could be short as three

LEAD: ♣5

Alex owes me a point or two. He does have good heart spots and that may have motivated him to bid again.

Three notrump is not my idea of a good matchpoint contract. I don't think I'd even want to be there at IMPs.

It's frustrating because eight tricks are so easy. The ninth will be harder. The most obvious place for a ninth trick is in clubs. If I make the normal play of the club nine, I can get a second club trick whenever West has led from Q10xxx or K10xxx.

220

There are two problems with this.

1. If I play the nine and it forces out the queen or king I will
    have to get a second club trick to come to nine tricks. If
    I return a club now, the defense may win and switch to
    spades.
2. If I play on hearts rather than clubs, the defenders will
    see I have eight tricks and they won't give me my ninth.

I don't think I can make three notrump by making the normal play in clubs. Instead I'm going to make the odd play of
putting up the jack at trick one. It will win 25% of the time
and I think this is a better chance than that the defenders will
misdefend.

I do this and when the jack holds I can scramble home with
nine winners. I remember to compliment Alex on his good two
notrump bid.

COMPLETE HAND

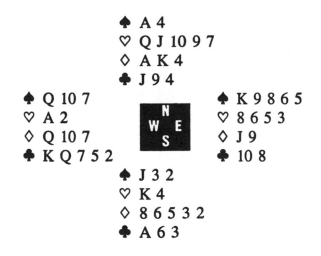

        ♠ A 4
        ♡ Q J 10 9 7
        ◊ A K 4
        ♣ J 9 4

♠ Q 10 7   ♠ K 9 8 6 5
♡ A 2   ♡ 8 6 5 3
◊ Q 10 7   ◊ J 9
♣ K Q 7 5 2   ♣ 10 8

        ♠ J 3 2
        ♡ K 4
        ◊ 8 6 5 3 2
        ♣ A 6 3

FURTHER ANALYSIS

You should not think of this club position as a fifty percent proposition. Even if you play the nine and East plays the king or queen, you are not completely safe. East could have both the king and queen. Example:

```
            J 9 4
10 8 7 5                 K Q 2
            A 6 3
```

Note that if your opponents were playing fourth best and they led the seven, if the nine forced the king or queen, you *would* be safe as long as West had led from his long suit. The rule of eleven would tell you East had only one higher card than the seven and he has just played it. If you play the nine (correctly) and East plays the ten, the rule of eleven would tell you that you had just misguessed and you won't have to wait until the end of the hand to find out.

```
            J 9 4
K 10 8 7                 Q 5 2
            A 6 3

            _____

            J 9 4
K Q 8 7                 10 5 2
            A 6 3
```

When West leads the seven, you know East has the K, the Q, or the 10. West won't have all three because he would lead the king. When you play dummy's nine, you find out instantly how your evening is going.

BOTH VULNERABLE
WEST DEALS

South
♠ A Q J 5 3
♡ K 7
◇ 9 6 2
♣ A 6 3

West, in first seat, opens ONE NOTRUMP showing 15 to 17. Alex passes and East bids THREE DIAMONDS which West alerts. These days you never know what to expect so I ask. Three diamonds is a natural and weak signoff.

The fact that the three diamonds is weak suggests I will find a few points in Alex's hand. The fact that I have three diamonds suggests Alex may be short in diamonds and can have some spade support. I venture THREE SPADES. It could work out awfully, but at matchpoints, it is a reasonable risk.

Opener bids FOUR DIAMONDS which confirms my hope for a singleton or void in Alex's hand. When Alex bids FOUR SPADES I am far more confident than when I bid three spades. East makes an unusual contribution to the auction. He bids FIVE DIAMONDS which is a peculiar action to take opposite a strong notrump opener.

Since I have good high cards but poor shape and only five spades, I DOUBLE. If East can make this it will be a fluke and we'll get no matchpoints anyway. What I can't afford here is to set them one and find a lot of other pairs are making 140 or 170.

It doesn't matter apparently because Alex pulls to FIVE SPADES. He wouldn't do this unless he expected to make it. Why would he save against a save?

Opener is busy thinking. Is he offended that we have bid to

five spades after a one notrump opening? Am I going to run into a double on principle?

No. Opener bids SIX DIAMONDS and Alex PASSES!

This is a sequence I have never heard before but I have no doubt it is a forcing pass. In spite of opener's 16 count, Alex is willing to have me bid six spades.

I have fourteen points, opener has sixteen, more or less, and East may have zero on upwards. This means Alex can have up to ten high cards plus a probable void in diamonds.

If Alex has:

♠ K x x x
♡ A J x x x
◊ —
♣ x x x x

I can get all thirteen tricks if the hearts are three-three with the queen onside. Or, opposite:

♠ K x x x
♡ x x x x
◊ —
♣ K J x x x

I may make six spades.

Without going into dozens of hands, it is clear that I can construct easy examples of seven or eight point hands which make bidding six spades the winning action.

I bid SIX SPADES not expecting it to be cold but it should be playable. West shows remarkable restrain and it gets passed out. West leads the king of diamonds.

BOTH VULNERABLE
WEST DEALS

♠ K 10 8 6 4 2
♡ A 8 6 2
◇ —
♣ J 9 4

```
    N
  W   E
    S
```

♠ A Q J 5 3
♡ K 7
◇ 9 6 2
♣ A 6 3

West	North	East	South
1NT	Pass	3◇ (a)	3♠
4◇	4♠	5◇	Double
Pass	5♠	Pass	Pass
6◇	Pass (b)	Pass	6♠
Pass	Pass	Pass	

(a) Weak
(b) Forcing pass

LEAD: ◇K

This is both a good and a bad dummy. It has a void and it has six trump but it has no fillers. If Alex had the jack of hearts instead of the jack of clubs, we would be on a near proven finesse.

As it is, I have a play. The problem is going to focus on the club suit. I don't expect West to have the KQ tight, but I do expect him to have the KQ and some number of clubs.

If so, I've got him.

The play is more or less predetermined. Ruff the diamond.

225

Draw two rounds of trump. Ruff a second diamond. Two rounds of hearts and a heart ruff in my hand. Ruff the last diamond. Ruff dummy's last heart.

Here's where we are:

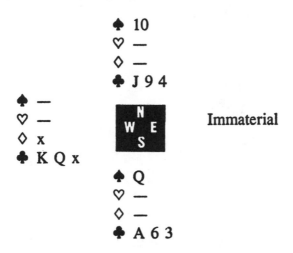

```
            ♠ 10
            ♡ —
            ◊ —
            ♣ J 9 4
♠ —
♡ —            N          Immaterial
◊ x          W   E
♣ K Q x        S
            ♠ Q
            ♡ —
            ◊ —
            ♣ A 6 3
```

When I lead low toward the jack, West wins the king but is endplayed. When he returns the club two I have no problem playing the jack. After all, if West didn't have both honors, wouldn't he let East win the trick to return a club?

COMPLETE HAND

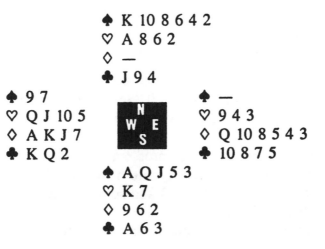

```
                  ♠ K 10 8 6 4 2
                  ♡ A 8 6 2
                  ◊ —
                  ♣ J 9 4
♠ 9 7                              ♠ —
♡ Q J 10 5          N              ♡ 9 4 3
◊ A K J 7         W   E            ◊ Q 10 8 5 4 3
♣ K Q 2             S              ♣ 10 8 7 5
                  ♠ A Q J 5 3
                  ♡ K 7
                  ◊ 9 6 2
                  ♣ A 6 3
```

FURTHER ANALYSIS

The play was uneventful. What was significant was the auction. It's worth looking at each person's decisions and noting how a competitive auction turned into a forcing sequence at the six level.

I would also tend to respect this particular West who was able to restrain himself at the end of our sequence and not double six spades.

His six diamond save might have gone for 800 had I led the king of hearts or perhaps the ace of clubs followed by a switch to hearts. But it was a reasonable effort. I think he was a little bit unlucky with the actual result.

50 HIGHLY-RECOMMENDED TITLES

FOR BEGINNERS
#0300 Future Champions' Bridge Series 9.95
#2130 Kantar-Introduction to Declarer's Play 7.00
#2135 Kantar-Introduction to Defender's Play 7.00
#0101 Stewart-Baron-The Bridge Book 1 .... 9.95
#1101 Silverman-Elementary Bridge
Five Card Major Student Text 2.75
#0660 Penick-Beginning Bridge Complete 8.95
#0661 Penick-Beginning Bridge Quizzes 6.95
#3230 Lampert-Fun Way to Serious Bridge 8.95

FOR ADVANCED PLAYERS
#2250 Reese-Master Play 4.95
#1420 Klinger-Modern Losing Trick Count 13.95
#2240 Love-Bridge Squeezes Complete 5.95
#0103 Stewart-Baron-The Bridge Book 3 .... 9.95
#0740 Woolsey-Matchpoints 14.95
#0741 Woolsey-Partnership Defense 9.95
#1702 Bergen-Competitive Auctions 9.95
#0636 Lawrence-Falsecards 9.95

BIDDING - 2 OVER 1 GAME FORCE
#4750 Bruno & Hardy-Two-Over-One Game Force:
An Introduction 9.95
#1750 Hardy-Two-Over-One Game Force 14.95
#1790 Lawrence-Workbook on the Two Over One System 11.95
#4525 Lawrence-Bidding Quizzes Book 1 .... 13.95

DEFENSE
#0520 Blackwood-Complete Book of Opening Leads 14.95
#3030 Ewen-Opening Leads 14.95
#0104 Stewart-Baron-The Bridge Book 4 .... 7.95
#0631 Lawrence-Dynamic Defense 11.95
#1200 Woolsey-Modern Defensive Signalling 4.95

FOR INTERMEDIATE PLAYERS
#2120 Kantar-Complete Defensive Bridge 20.00
#3015 Root-Commonsense Bidding 14.00
#0630 Lawrence-Card Combinations 12.95
#0102 Stewart-Baron-The Bridge Book 2 .... 9.95
#1102 Silverman-Intermediate Bridge Five
      Card Major Student Text 2.95
#0575 Lampert-The Fun Way to Advanced Bridge 11.95
#0633 Lawrence-How to Read Your Opponents' Cards 9.95
#3672 Truscott-Bid Better, Play Better 11.00
#1765 Lawrence-Judgment at Bridge 9.95

PLAY OF THE HAND
#2150 Kantar-Test your Bridge Play, Vol. 1 .... 7.00
#3675 Watson-Watson's Classic Book on
      the Play of the Hand 12.00
#1932 Mollo-Gardener-Card Play Technique 12.95
#3009 Root-How to Play a Bridge Hand 12.00
#1104 Silverman-Play of the Hand as
      Declarer and Defender 2.95
#2175 Truscott-Winning Declarer Play 10.00
#3803 Sydnor-Bridge Made Easy Book 3 .... 6.00

CONVENTIONS
#2115 Kantar-Bridge Conventions 10.00
#0610 Kearse-Bridge Conventions Complete 24.95
#3011 Root-Pavlicek-Modern Bridge Conventions 15.00
#0240 Championship Bridge Series (All 36) 25.95

DUPLICATE STRATEGY
#1600 Klinger-50 Winning Duplicate Tips 12.95
#2260 Sheinwold-Duplicate Bridge 3.95

FOR ALL PLAYERS
#3889 Darvas & de V. Hart-Right Through The Pack 12.95
#0790 Simon: Why You Lose at Bridge 11.95
#4850 Encyclopedia of Bridge, Official (ACBL) 39.95

DEVYN PRESS INC.

3600 Chamberlain Lane, Suite 230, Louisville, KY 40241

1-800-274-2221

CALL TOLL FREE IN THE U.S. & CANADA
TO ORDER OR TO REQUEST OUR 64 PAGE
FULL COLOR CATALOG OF BRIDGE BOOKS,
SUPPLIES AND GIFTS.

Lawrence & Hanson WINNING BRIDGE INTANGIBLES .... $ 4.95
Lipkin INVITATION TO ANNIHILATION .... $ 8.95
Michaels & Cohen 4-3-2-1 MANUAL .... $ 2.95
Penick BEGINNING BRIDGE COMPLETE .... $ 8.95
Penick BEGINNING BRIDGE QUIZZES... $ 6.95
Powell TICKETS TO THE DEVIL.. $ 5.95
Reese & Hoffman PLAY IT AGAIN, SAM .... $ 7.95
Rosenkranz
    BRIDGE: THE BIDDER'S GAME $12.95
    TIPS FOR TOPS .... $ 9.95
    MORE TIPS FOR TOPS .... $ 9.95
    TRUMP LEADS .... $ 7.95
    OUR MAN GODFREY.. $10.95
Rosenkranz & Alder BID TO WIN, PLAY FOR PLEASURE $11.95
Rosenkranz & Truscott BIDDING ON TARGET $10.95
Silverman
    ELEMENTARY BRIDGE FIVE CARD MAJOR STUDENT TEXT ...... $ 2.75
    INTERMEDIATE BRIDGE FIVE CARD MAJOR STUDENT TEXT .... $ 2.95
    ADVANCED & DUPLICATE BRIDGE STUDENT TEXT .... $ 2.95
    PLAY OF THE HAND AS DECLARER
    & DEFENDER STUDENT TEXT .... $ 2.95
Simon
    WHY YOU LOSE AT BRIDGE $11.95
Stewart & Baron
    THE BRIDGE BOOK, Vol. 1, Beginning .... $ 9.95
    THE BRIDGE BOOK, Vol. 2, Intermediate .... $ 9.95
    THE BRIDGE BOOK, Vol. 3, Advanced .... $ 9.95
    THE BRIDGE BOOK, Vol. 4, Defense .... $ 7.95
Thomas SHERLOCK HOLMES, BRIDGE DETECTIVE .... $ 9.95
Von Elsner
    THE ACE OF SPIES .... $ 5.95
    CRUISE BRIDGE .... $ 5.95
    EVERYTHING JAKE WITH ME .... $ 5.95
    THE BEST OF JAKE WINKMAN .... $ 5.95
    THE JAKE OF HEARTS .... $ 5.95
    THE JAKE OF DIAMONDS .... $ 5.95
Woolsey
    MATCHPOINTS $14.95
    MODERN DEFENSIVE SIGNALLING .... $ 4.95
    PARTNERSHIP DEFENSE .... $ 9.95
World Bridge Federation APPEALS COMMITTEE DECISIONS
    from the 1994 NEC WORLD CHAMPIONSHIPS .... $ 9.95